SOLACE

SOLACE

A MEMOIR

CORNELIA MAUDE SPELMAN

JACKLEG PRESS

JackLeg Press
jacklegpress.org

Cornelia Maude Spelman
corneliaspelman.com

Printed in the United States of America.
ISBN: 978-1956907162

Library of Congress Control Number: 2023945761

Cover design and layout by K. M. Weber, I Libri Book Design
Edited by David Wesley Williams

For Reg

and for Sam and Kate

Those into whose lives you are born do not pass
away. You bear them with you, as you hope to
be borne by those who come after you.

—J.M. Coetzee

Who, if I cried out, would hear me
among the hierarchies of angels?

—Rainer Maria Rilke

CONTENTS

SOLACE

A Letter to My Mother

PART ONE

Dear Mother,

It's 5:30 in the morning, nearly thirty-two years after you died. I couldn't sleep. I had to get up and start writing. I've been lying in bed composing this letter to you, sighing, and trying my meditation breathing (that usually works to put me back to sleep) and even, I'm afraid, waking my husband by cuddling next to him. His warmth is comforting. He's warm, as I am— alive. But you've been cold, gone, dead, for so long now.

Yet . . . the Buddhists say, if you want to see your ancestors, all you need to do is look at your own hand, your own body. So you are here, Mother—in my eyes, my hair. In the way I write this sentence. Generations are here, living within me.

Mother, if you could see my children—your grandson, named for your father, and your granddaughter, named for you. You and your father and your mother live on in my son and daughter, too. My son looks like your father. The same pronounced eyebrows—the nose—the whole look about his face. And he, too, is "sunny." Everyone likes him, just as every-one liked your father, whose popularity I read about in your old hometown newspaper. Isn't that something?

And your granddaughter. Smart and beautiful—more beautiful than your mother (she would be jealous, probably) —but her politics would make your mother turn over in her grave. She, like me, like you, is one of "those Dems" your mother scorned.

But there's so much to say, Mother, about my son and daughter. Thirty-two years have passed, and so I can't say everything, or I'd be writing for the rest of my life. I hope mine is longer than yours was. I'm in my sixtieth year, approaching the age you were when you died. If I were to die, as you did at sixty-three, I'd only have three years left to live. I'd like a lot

3

more years than that, though I don't know if I'll get them. If I don't, it won't be because I wanted to die, like you, or because I damaged my body, like you did. No. Your horrifying example helped me. I (finally!) quit smoking. I quit drinking. At my age you were in and out of hospitals, but I am well. I walk each day. I breathe freely. My skin is fresh; I have few wrinkles. That cigarette smoke ruined your lovely skin.

I suppose I could thank you, Mother, for your bad example. It seared me, watching you destroy yourself. While it still took me longer than it should have to quit smoking, I wanted more not to end up like you did, than to smoke. In a way, l had to abandon you, to be healthy when you weren't. I remember, when (finally!) I was able to stop smoking, how I struggled with you in my mind, how I had to say, "No, Mother! I *won't* be like you! I *will* be healthy! I must live differently than you did—I must renounce your ways. I'm sorry to leave you behind. But it's me or you. And I have children who need me."

It was my daughter's crying, at ten, when I had smoked again after having quit again, that drove me to quit for good. "Please, Mommy, please don't smoke!" she'd cried. And I'd heard her, knowing exactly how she felt, knowing, too, how you must have felt, disgusted with yourself, when I'd cried, in my twenties, the same plea, but you hadn't quit. And didn't. And died because of it.

What made the difference, Mother? Why couldn't you, and why could I?

Maybe it was because I got just enough more love, as a child, than you had. Because *you* were my mother. You were not able to love me as I needed and wanted you to. I believe this was because when your beloved father died, you froze a part of yourself—yet you must have given me enough love to keep me going, to give me the strength I needed, to stop smoking, to extricate myself from my first two bad marriages, to get sober.

Somebody loved me enough. And I haven't thought it was my father, your husband—why did we call him by his first name, Mother, and never "Father" or "Daddy"? Did he not

4

want to be a father? Like your mother, who did not want to be a grandmother and so we called her, too, by her first name?

On the back of one of the few photographs of me as a baby, in your handwriting, you had written "The best baby in Jackson County." Such is my inheritance—a few scrawled words. But, if I was the best baby, perhaps I made it easier for you.

You were never mean, like your mother was to you, nor critical of me. You did not pay enough attention to me, but I knew you wished me well—when you thought of me. I guess, sad though that seems, it was enough for me to survive on. Well, that was all a long, long time ago, Mother.

Where shall I begin, to tell you?

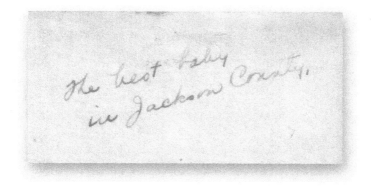

Episode 1

Alcohol

By the time I was thirty, I had been worried about my drinking for a dozen years.

It seemed strange to me that what began with the idea of having a cocktail before dinner (a grown-up, civilized, innocent, commonplace thing to do), a Manhattan, Mother's favorite, carefully measured with the silver jigger made to look like a very big thimble, then poured into the crystal green-stemmed glass which, along with the jigger, I had inherited from my grandmother; its liquid glowing a honeyed gold, with a maraschino cherry resting on the bottom — it seemed strange that this idea of the pretty drink would "somehow" end up with me drunk, saying and doing things I would regret, endangering myself (and others) if I drove, which, at times, I did, one eye closed to better see the white center line on a country road; at times, falling down, and by a miracle not hitting my head, nearly daily suffering the dry mouth, throbbing headache, and general misery of hangovers, or even having no memory of what I had done the night before.

Why did "it" keep happening when my intention had been just to "have a drink"? I thought of it that way — that "it" was "happening," and I could not yet see that I was the actor, the person who made "it" happen; and yet, it did not happen to everyone. It seemed that others—not by any means all, since by that time I was married to a heavy drinker—could have that nice cocktail in a pretty glass, admire it, enjoy it, and stop. Or maybe even have another, but then stop. Why couldn't I?

I really knew nothing at that time about alcoholism. An *alcoholic*, I thought, if I thought about it at all, was a man lying drunk in the street. I was thirty years old, healthy, mother of a little son, educated.

True, I had heard my father tell the story of his father—a dentist whose specialty was repairing the jaws of men kicked by horses, and a binge drinker, who had once locked himself into the garage with a loaded shotgun, necessitating my half-grown father to call the police. But that was long before I was born. It had nothing to do with me.

True, I had heard vague comments about my oldest brother, the one who disappeared and about whom I wrote in my memoir, *Missing*, having had, among other serious issues, problems with alcohol. But that, too, had nothing to do with me.

True, I was aware that certain members of my family often "drank too much," got argumentative, maudlin, nasty—or sometimes very funny—but they weren't *alcoholic*, weren't like that drunk man lying in the street. Everyone I knew drank, some of them more than I did. But I was, deep down, worried about my drinking. I knew there was something different about my interest in, my "relationship with," alcohol.

Back when I was twenty-six, already divorced after that brief early marriage and raising my son alone, I'd found a counselor at a local mental health center and in the course of talking with her about my loneliness and unhappiness (it was two years before Mother smoked herself to death), I had shared my worries about my drinking. "If your hostess put a bottle of wine on the table, would you need to pick it up?" she'd asked me. "Of course not," I'd replied, and she'd said, "Well, you're not an alcoholic." Later, of course, I saw that she was as ignorant of alcoholism as I was—alcoholism is not, unfortunately, a required course in

8

mental health educations—but I was only too glad to have a professional tell me not to worry. But I did continue to worry.

Five years later, and into that second marriage, I made an appointment with a trained alcohol counselor, recommended by my best friend, to talk about my husband's drinking. The alcohol counselor listened, and then asked me to tell her about my own drinking, which I did. "If you want someone to tell you not to worry about your drinking," she said, friendly but no-nonsense, "you'll have to find someone else, because I am telling you that you are right to worry about it." She loaned me books and pamphlets about alcoholism, and that night, after I'd put my little son to bed, I'd poured some scotch into a glass to keep me company as I read them.

Reading what she loaned me, and then talking with her in more sessions, I learned that I was not too young or too healthy to be an alcoholic. And she said something that enabled me to utterly change my life (and the lives of my son and future daughter): she said alcoholism was like an elevator and I could get off at any floor. That drunk man lying on the street whom I had visualized as a "real" alcoholic was at the end of the elevator ride, on the bottom.

I did not have to ride the elevator all the way down.

I learned that my episodes of forgetting what I had done the night before had a name: alcoholic blackouts. And the "it" that I had not understood was alcoholism, something I could manage, like a disease, which is the simplest way for me to view alcoholism. I could see myself in everything I read about alcoholism, and I could see the road ahead if I did not stop drinking. My own behavior while drinking had illustrated, vividly, the ugliness of repetitive drunkenness. I did not want to be like that —or even worse. Here was a way—stopping drinking—to save myself from "it."

But I was "only" thirty years old. What about the whole life ahead of me?—weddings and parties and champagne, and those beautiful green crystal glasses filled with the glow of a Manhattan, its magnified cherry on the bottom; what about the salted rim of a chilled Margarita glass? How was I to live without ever having a drink again? Because my counselor and the literature she'd provided to me made it crystal-clear that the only way for me to stop "it" was not to drink. Alcohol was, for me, poison. I must not have one drink, ever, of any sort. She explained that alcoholism was progressive, and progressed even when you didn't drink. She told of people who hadn't had a drink in many years yet again had become captive, had even proceeded to die from it, when, believing themselves cured, had again begun to drink.

And then, one evening in May, the counselor took me to my first Alcoholics Anonymous meeting, this particular meeting a fairly long drive from my small town in New Hampshire into another even smaller town in our neighboring state of Vermont. The honesty, good cheer, and friendliness of this "fellowship," especially the laughter, often over the most painful or embarrassing things, was a tonic. I saw and heard from others who had also experienced "it," and were living examples of how to change, how to escape the dangerous cycle—living examples of what I learned to call *Sobriety*: not drinking, one day at a time, facing reality and being completely honest ("My name is Cornelia and I am an alcoholic"), making amends, turning to others for help and helping others, going to meetings, and a lot of simple but very useful slogans ("people who don't go to meetings don't hear what happens to people who don't go to meetings").

I loved that meeting, and I thought I would go home and have a drink and think about it. But we took a wrong way on that dark country road, and by the time we got to my house, it was very late. I decided I wouldn't, after all, have that drink.

One day at a time, thanks to my fellow alcoholics and thousands of meetings, I have not had another one. Not having another one is what has made it possible for me to live the life I am writing about in this memoir. Being sober has been the key to every day of every year since that first momentous AA meeting.

Episode 2

Returning

I hear the resonant, melancholy chime of a clock here in the spare and empty lobby of this old Vermont inn, where I have been sitting for the past hour, at a smooth wooden table, soothing to my hand, with a cup of coffee and a single lamp burning, writing in my diary, with my blue fountain pen. The tall wooden counter of this 1797 stage-coach inn thoughtfully holds a modern one-cup coffee machine, little tubs of cream, a green, cut-glass sugar bowl and packets of sweetener, so that any guest, like me, who is up early and needs her cup, can descend the stairs from her room, make coffee, and sit in perfect peace in this tranquil, clean, old-fashioned, somehow courteous room with its wing-back chairs and its graceful brass chandelier.

The clock strikes six times. Soon the serene-faced woman on the inn's staff who walks quietly about—an older woman, like me—will be coming in, and I think, "That is the chime of Time, and everything I have always been writing about in my diaries is about Time, its passing, and my going back into it and wresting from it an understanding of my years and of what my time on this earth has been about."

On this trip, ten years after I began writing my letter to Mother, I'm visiting those small towns in New Hampshire and its neighbor, Vermont, in which my most formative adult years were passed—years that included the births of my son and my daughter, two marriages and two divorces, the illnesses and deaths both of Mother and of my best friend, my finding sobriety, and meeting my husband, with whom I have spent the past decades in love, and in love's struggles. This trip will likely be my last visit to these places, my last return to those times spent here.

Those times that are long over, long past, and yet, perhaps only because I had left my old places and hadn't seen them day-to-day, hadn't seen them for years, for decades—these old places seem to have kept alive in them those times I spent there, as if in a movie that I could watch again, except I am the only one who sees it.

This final visit has been filled with these ghosts of my past, and I am ready, finally, to leave them, to leave the past behind. Now the past is by far most of my life—three-score and ten years to ponder as I keep moving in the stream of Time into my shorter and shorter future, towards the end of my own story. How is it, I wonder, that I didn't ever really understand that the past never comes back?

And yet—I *am* bringing it back, in writing.

Episode 3

The Necklace of Luminous Stones

It was October, and I'd been sober for three-and-a-half years. I dreamt of an unusual necklace. It was intricately fashioned of silver and round, luminous stones, unlike any I'd ever seen. I could have it if I wanted it. I woke, to the crying of my one-and-a-half-year-old daughter, before I could decide.

I dreamt often of jewelry—finding it and losing it. I knew my dreams had to be as important as the heart that was beating, slippery and strong, within my chest. Sometimes when I would talk about my dreams with my best friend, I would have a sense of discovery, but then I'd get distracted by daily life. Changing my daughter's diapers, retrieving my ten-year-old son's rolled-up discarded socks and scattered toys, buying milk, eggs, butter, hamburger—the treadmill of my life took precedence.

In my neighborhood in my small town in New Hampshire, I had a few favorite trees. One of them, a maple, had turned red instead of yellow that fall. I'm sure that in past autumns it was yellow, because I'd photographed it, trying to capture its beauty. Was red its true color, and the yellow years its years of ripening? Was it ill?

Another favorite tree, the maple across the street in my neighbor's front yard, had turned its usual color, a vivid orange—all the shades of orange in my son's giant-size Crayola crayon box: those perfect pointed sticks of color named rusty-gold, maize, mahogany, burnt sienna, and bittersweet. Yet, how melancholy those colors seemed that fall. My best friend, born only one day apart and the same year as me, had breast cancer. I was afraid for her. And I was afraid for myself; I could not stay in a marriage in which I was sober and my husband thought my sobriety foolish, thought that his own drinking was not a problem.

My favorite trees reminded me, in my headlong fall through life, of the season, the place, my external life, although my interior was hidden. My son and I watched a television program that showed the interior of the body captured by tiny cameras placed inside it. We saw blood coursing through veins, vocal cords striking one another, and a ruptured aneurysm—the blood spewing into the brain, pieces of brain tissue floating about like cotton candy. My hidden feelings were like that aneurysm.

When my children were infants, I had difficulty distinguishing them from myself. I would wake, at times, hearing their thin, dependent cries before they had actually begun to cry. I knew the cord had been cut between us; at both births I had watched it being cut, yet my son and my daughter remained, for a time, as connected to me as if that splendid, bluish, muscular cord still stretched from their small bodies back into my own.

That fall, however, as my son, at ten, acquired the faint odor of approaching adolescence, and my one-and-a-half-year-old daughter proclaimed her first words, I could sometimes forget their existence. After a few hours of separation they could startle me. When had they arrived, and how long had they been here? Where had the child (me) pictured in my parents' family album gone?

I was sending my daughter for a few hours each morning to nursery school so I could write, trying to begin a novel, leaving the tumult of my household so I could sit at the old, scuffed, wooden desk in a corner of the room that had the most windows, which were filled with the sad October sun. The egg-encrusted plates, the dusty tabletops, the unmade beds, did not claim me on those mornings.

It was only a few weeks after that dream of the necklace when I dreamt about it again. Inside a shop, it was being saved especially for me. "Try it on! You must try it on!" said the shopkeeper. I knew I couldn't afford it, but I picked it up, fastened it, and it settled, with a sweet weight, around my neck, its white stones glowing.

Episode 4

Somewhere I Used to Call Home

FROM MY DIARY:

The summer after my dream of that beautiful necklace of luminous stones, I was accepted at a writer's conference in Vermont.

I began getting up every morning before the children were awake to write, in earnest, a diary:

In a few weeks, I'll be writing every morning not here at my desk, but in my room at the conference. There's bound to be a lot of drinking. My AA sponsor tells me there will be at least one other person there from AA, probably even more, and I should just put a note on the bulletin board to arrange an AA meeting. I'm not worried. I don't want to drink. I know what would happen, how it would ruin everything.

I will be free just to write, to listen to readings, to talk about books and writing. This morning, writing in my diary, facing this quiet, attentive, empty, listening page, I see it is a much better way to start off the day than a sink full of last night's dirty dishes. I'll do those later.

I have the feeling I had as a child when we left on our one-and-only family vacation, to Canada. Excitement. The scent of the new blue jeans Mother had gotten me for the trip. I guess I think of this because I'm up early, or maybe the feeling is more like the first day of school—having to get up early and get going, after those generous leisurely mornings of summer.

My in-laws are visiting, staying at the motel in a nearby town. After my father-in-law had a few drinks, he recited those lines "Grow old along with me, the best is yet to be," which pleased my mother-in-law so much because it was rare evidence of a heart. She told me in the kitchen, "Dad loves his job, the children, football, then me. Well, that's love!" She thinks my going to AA meetings and saying I am alcoholic is some kind of strange, embarrassing idea I have. Of course, my husband thinks the same. She and my father-in-law like their cocktails, and her son can do no wrong. She disapproves of my going to the writers' conference; she thinks I'm wrong to do anything other than stay at home. She asks how her son can work and take care of the kids. I want to say to her, but of course I don't, "Well, I work and take care of the kids all the time," and I'd like to add, but of course I don't, "No, you never left your children in order to go to a conference, never left them to go to work, never left them at all, and still, they left you because you locked them in a suffocating embrace, and now you are locked out of their adult lives. You prefer living in the past. You're always looking through their baby albums, always telling the same childhood stories, and have not managed to forge relationships with them as adults. No one is happy when you come to visit."

She said to my husband, "Oh, I saw you before you saw yourself!" when he tried to cover his nakedness after she walked into our bedroom one morning without knocking.

In the coffee shop in town, yesterday, the sight of a baby struck me with a tender blow. She was very new, wrapped in her receiving blanket like a loaf of French bread, the way they do in the hospital. Her head was small enough to cup in your hand, and she looked like a baby robin that had fallen out of its nest, blind and helpless. Her mother, blooming with vitality and milk, gazed lovingly at her, smiling. For an instant, I wanted it all again. But I am past my season of babies, despite the allure.

I slept late, have a headache, and a black mood waiting off stage. I may menstruate; I hope so, then I can blame all my weakness of character on my biology. My little daughter woke me several times last night, and I guessed by the smell of her breath that she is getting sick. I feel responsible for her cold, as if the reason she is getting sick is that I am going to the conference. I woke up tired and cranky. And when my husband cracked, sarcastically, "I thought you wanted to get up early every morning to *write*," I looked for something to throw at him but couldn't find anything soft enough. My daughter's small face appeared and she whispered, "Better, Mommy," and patted me, and told her father, "Mommy better." Actually, Mommy felt like a big jerk. My husband said, "I guess you haven't gotten your period yet." I wanted to run out of the house, but where would I go?

The air up here on the Vermont mountains, surrounded by a national forest, is like the air of heaven. You feel removed from real life up here, suddenly dropped into a crowd of several hundred mostly young people who are excited and eager to be here writing and reading. Naturally, in this environment, the men are eager for more than writing and reading; many of the women, too. In the afternoon sun, several of the men were crowding around me. I like one, in particular.

I've been sitting in some of the talks and readings with my new pals, including that particular man, who has an intelligent face, gentle blue eyes, and a tangle of brown curly hair. He's quiet, and often takes out a pocket-size notebook to write something in it. His hands are large and look smooth; very different from my husband's rough, cracked, carpenter's hands. When we were sitting side-by-side at one of the readings, my leg was lightly touching his, and I didn't move it away. In the barn, where social events for the conference are held, he played old, romantic tunes on the piano. Those are my songs! I know the words to nearly all of them, and sing them to myself or to the children.

At the end of these first five days of the conference, my husband and the children came up to spend one night, then returned home while I finished the last five days here. My son has never seen me among so many other people. He sees me only at home, as Mom. My daughter's small, suntanned foot was sticking out of the portable crib where she slept, and I cried, looking at it, wishing that my husband would take me in his arms, tell me of course he would stop drinking, that I was more important, and keep me from falling over this cliff I'm on. But he didn't. He just went to sleep.

I returned home today, shaky from love and the decongestant tablets I've been taking for this bad cold I have. A hot, still, slumbering August day; nothing changed, but everything changed. I woke from a nap, weeping, having dreamt that it all hadn't really happened; my new friends, the excitement of being with people whose interests are like mine; but most of all, this man and me, our deep connection. When I told him the story of finding sobriety, of my children and the details of my daughter's birth,

25

I cried. Will I ever see him again? In the confusion of waking from a daytime nap, I didn't even know where I was—somewhere I used to call home.

⌒

We were in the kitchen, and snips of my husband's golden hair—it really was golden, a natural blonde with streaks of a warm honey color—floated down to the scuffed linoleum floor as I cut it with a sharp small pair of scissors I use for sewing.

My husband said, "I guess this is the last time you're going to cut my hair," in a tone of voice that showed me he was making kind of a joke of it, not wanting to feel whatever it is he was feeling. What I was feeling was disbelief—that this scene of apparent domestic comfort and intimacy was just brutally false, the air in our kitchen heavy with loss.

The snips of golden hair that were falling to the floor were the hopes of a happy family with him and with my eleven-year-old-son and our daughter, two-and-a-half years old. She was watching the haircut, sitting on the short wooden stool I sometimes used for her to stand on at the old white ceramic sink for waterplay.

I told my husband last night I am leaving, with the children, moving to Illinois to be with the man to whom I felt so connected.

⌒

The next year and a half, back and forth between Illinois and New Hampshire, would be very hard.

Episode 5

If I Kiss You a Thousand Times

In New Hampshire, in my best friend's house, I carried the flowers in front of me like a shield into the den, now made into her room. A hospital bed and wheelchair occupied the space she'd cleared only a few months earlier for a new sofa.

I was disappointed that there were already a number of bouquets in the room, many with the florists' small tags still attached. I wanted mine to be the only one. I put my flowers—a purple anemone; waxy yellow, fragrant freesias; and a creamy pink rose—closest to her. She raised her eyebrows in acknowledgment.

Illness had made the flesh of her face taut across the bones, had reduced her, altogether, to a smaller version of herself. But her hands were unchanged; they were the hands of a young woman, with long, strong nails painted pink. She wore, besides her wedding band, a tourmaline ring whose bluish-green color I'd admired many times. I felt relief at the sight of her hands, like a lost child finally seeing his mother's face. Sitting down beside her, I lifted one hand and kissed it lightly.

She looked straight ahead. She said, "What's happening in the outside world?"

"Oh, not much," I said. "The snow is melting. Your drive-way's full of mud. It feels a little like spring."

She turned her head on the pillow to look at me. Her eyes were so blue. She closed one.

"You look pretty," I told her. "Your cheeks are pink, you just look . . . pretty."

"Not like a dying woman, huh?" She had to say it.

The phone rang, and I moved it so she could pick it up her-self. My foot knocked against a box of photographs lying next to the bed, so I picked up the box and began looking through it. Her voice on the phone was languid, sleepy.

"Oh, I'm okay. Don't worry about me. The doctors say I have maybe a couple of weeks left. It's okay. We just have to accept it. I'm not in pain, really, I'm just drowsy from the drugs, so if I nod off while I'm talking to you, don't be offended." She made a noise like a chuckle, and then was silent. I glanced at her.

"Uh huh. Uh huh." Her look of worry was faint, as if it was a feeling she couldn't quite remember. "Oh, don't cry," she said to the phone. She could have been talking to a child who'd scraped a knee. "I love you, too," she said.

She hung up the phone, looked at me and sighed heavily. "My aunt." I nodded.

"This is hard on her," she said. I nodded again.

I said, "You sound . . . are you feeling better about this today?"

She closed her eyes and breathed deeply, said, "I know it sounds crazy, but I'm kind of looking forward to it, in a way. I'm sort of . . . curious."

I looked at her, trying to memorize her face. Then I returned to looking through the photographs. They made a dry, papery, sliding sound in the room. I thought she had fallen asleep, and was startled when I looked up to see one of her eyes open. I held out a photograph of a baby, said, "Is this you? I can't tell if it's you or your daughter."

Her daughter was six; I remembered when my friend was pregnant with her, wearing an old fur coat that wouldn't button across her belly. We'd been standing next to a shelf of cereals in the grocery store, her dark, glossy hair full around her face, which was rosy and healthy.

She took the photograph, squinting at it because she had lost clear vision in one eye. "That's me," she said. She looked at it for a long moment. "That's a beautiful child, isn't it?" she said, as though she were looking at a picture of someone else.

I laughed, frightened. "Of course you were! You're still beautiful."

She held out her hand for another photo. I gave her a recent one of her and her husband, leaning together in the sun in front of their old farmhouse. She looked sad in the photo, as if her gaze went past the lens of the camera, into the future, into this room. "That was after my hair grew back," she said, handing the photo back to me and closing her eye.

I was studying the photos for the proof they offered that she'd lived unaware, ordinary moments: here she was in her dorm room at college; here, at a wedding; here, posing sideways to show her pregnant silhouette. This pretty woman I saw in the photos in a turquoise dress, the slender silver strap of an evening purse over her tanned arm, had become this invalid, lying in this bed.

I wished we could wonder over this together. I almost said my thought out loud but when I looked up I saw I'd forgotten: it was just me, now, wondering. She had let it go; she'd let it all go.

I came across a photo of us, taken a few years earlier. People said we looked alike, which pleased us; like sisters, almost twins, and in fact we had been born only one day apart. We didn't look at all alike, I suddenly decided—it was just our height, our dark hair. I thought of her voice a year earlier on the phone, high and frightened: "My hair's falling out! My pillow was covered with it this morning! I'm shedding like an animal!" I had nodded dumbly, staring at the Chiquita banana stickers plastered all over my kitchen phone.

I couldn't say, "Wake up! It's just a bad dream!" I couldn't say anything.

I came to feel that my own abundant hair had become an affront. I had bound it back when I'd visited her in the hospital, and I'd worn a baggy shirt to hide my breasts. But I couldn't make it up to her. It was as if a poisoned arrow had whistled past

31

me and lodged in her. I had to move cautiously toward her, past my own good fortune—my health—which separated us.

She'd only said it once, when I didn't expect it. We were having coffee together in town, anchoring ourselves in a conversation about clothes. I had shown her a sweater I'd bought, pleased by the sale price and the color. Leaning back as if to brace herself, she looked at it, then at me, blowing out her breath in a long sigh. "Lucky *you*," she'd said.

⌐

I heard the volume on the TV go up in the other room. Her daughter and my four-year-old daughter were watching cartoons. Her two-year-old son, naked from the waist down, came straggling into his mother's room. She opened both eyes. "Where are your pants?" she asked.

He grinned, and climbed onto her bed, ferreting down under the covers with her. She winced as he wiggled about. "Lie still," she said, "you'll hurt Mommy. Just lie still, darling."

I rose. "Come with me, okay?" I said. "Let's go see what the girls are doing." He looked questioningly at this mother, and she nodded to him. I picked him up and carried him into the other room, partly closing the door behind me. I could hear her settle down into her bed and sigh.

Her little son squirmed out of my arms and ran over to the girls on the sofa. He must have wandered away from his father upstairs and made his way down the steps; I heard his father's footsteps cross a room upstairs. I sat on the sofa for a moment, staring at the television, at the little girls' frail necks. I couldn't think what I should do.

Tea, I decided. I put the kettle on to boil and stood with my hands spread out flat on my friend's deep-red countertop, remembering when she'd showed me the color sample for it. For once, the booming voice of the cartoon character Fred Flintstone on the TV comforted me. When I turned to get milk, I saw the refrigerator was covered with her daughter's drawings, held on by magnets. She'd drawn a portrait of her family in which she'd given her mother, holding hands with her brother and father, lots of curly hair and a bright red smile that covered half the circle of her face. She'd drawn herself on the far side of her father. She'd made herself much bigger than her mother; she looked like a giant. Beneath this drawing was a card she'd made. In printing so careful it must have been coached, she'd written, "Dear Mommy, I'm sorry you have cancer. I hope you feel better soon."

My friend's husband came into the kitchen as I was reading his daughter's card, and I turned to him, ready to cry out in sorrow, but stopped when I saw his closed face, and I moved away from him to take the kettle off. "Want some tea?" I asked.

We'd never been at ease with each other. When the course of my friend's illness became clear, I'd taken him to lunch, hoping for his confidences. He'd talked of business, of mutual friends. When at last I had asked, "Have you thought about how you'll manage, with the children?" he'd looked as if I'd slapped him, then he'd looked away, warning me, "No. Should I?"

We sat in the kitchen with our tea. Her little son was there, with his pants back on, and he crawled onto my lap, dragging his blanket behind him. I held his bare foot in my hand, stroking it, and he lay back in my arms, gazing sleepily at my face. The child moved one hand dreamily over my breasts.

His father pointed out the window toward the yard. "I'm going to be able to get the garden in before too long," he said. I thought of the times my friend had brought bags of lettuce, squash, and tomatoes to me; of her strong, brisk stride up the uneven flagstones to my front door. Their garden the previous year had been large; when my friend first got sick, her friends tended it in shifts.

"Are you going to put in corn this year?" I asked her husband. I was watching her son fondle his blanket—his eyes were closing, as his father talked on about the garden. I suddenly held up my hand to stop him. I thought my friend—his wife—had called out. Gently I passed his son to him and tiptoed to her door.

I opened it slightly and peeked in. She waved. "I'm hungry. Do you think you could fix me some lunch?" she asked.

"Of course. What do you want? How about a BLT?" I said.

"Oh, that'd be lovely. And some hot tea?" she answered.

"Coming right up!" I said.

We'd had so many lunches together. Lunch was an excuse to talk; a time we could reserve for each other, the time furthest removed from our "real" lives of children, husbands, and work.

After the surgeon had removed her breast, and it seemed the news was good, I had brought lunch to her in the hospital. I'd stopped outside her door, leaning against the wall to put on my tap shoes, which I'd last used in a community theatre production a few years earlier. I'd knocked.

"Who's there?" she'd called.

I'd tap-danced into her room, carrying a tray and a white napkin over my arm.

After the second operation, I'd come in quietly with a sandwich and a chocolate milkshake. There'd been a tumor on her
brain—in a good spot, the surgeon had said—and he'd been able
to remove it. She'd worn a stocking cap over her shaved head,
and when I'd kissed her cheek I'd thought she'd cringed.

"How are *you*?" she'd insisted. I hadn't wanted to talk about
how I was. It would be like talking about the weather to someone
pinned under a truck. But I'd seen that she needed me to talk,
needed to act as if this was just another lunch. What I wished
I could have talked about was my divorce, my children, my ex-
panding new life-to-be in Illinois with the man I'd fallen in love
with at the writer's conference—a life that was not going to be
part of hers, anymore.

But she'd needed me to talk, so I had just nattered on, pretending we were just having lunch as usual, until finally she had
interrupted, putting her hands to her head, and crying, "I don't
care, anymore! I don't care about my hair, or being the best at
something, or being beautiful! I just want to be with my husband and my babies; I just want to *live!*"

Months later, over lunch, she'd said, "I have this stupid pain in
my hip. I finally told the doctor about it. I have to have a bone
scan. Would you go with me? It doesn't hurt, it's just that it scares
me. They put this machine over your body and your face."

I'd noticed her limping. I hadn't said anything about it. As
I started to say, "Of course!" she had leaned towards me, over
her half-eaten omelet. We'd floated on the noise of the busy
restaurant. "If this is another tumor, that's it, you know," she'd
said, as she'd waved to a friend across the room. She pointed to
her new skirt and sweater. "What will I do with the clothes I just
bought?"

35

During the scan, I'd talked too much, holding her hand. When the machine closed over her face, she'd squeezed my hand, hard, silencing me. I saw the outline of her skull twinkling in green lights on the monitor, then the long bones of her arms and legs, the perfect shape of her womanly pelvis.

After it was over, she'd joked, "I'm radioactive, stand back!"

A few days later, she'd learned that the scan showed a tumor on her hip, and, also, three more in her brain. At some point after that, we had had what would be our last lunch at a restaurant. I was to have met her at her office, but when I'd arrived, the door was closed. I'd knocked anxiously, saying in a low voice, "It's me. Are you okay?"

After a moment she'd opened the door, bent over in pain, then sunk quickly back into her chair, her head in her hands. "This goddamn headache!"

"Let me rub your neck," I'd offered.

She'd torn off her wig and scarf. Her odd new hair, almost blonde, barely covered her scalp and was as fine as a newborn baby's. I'd begun rubbing her neck and shoulders. After a while she'd said, "You know that woman from school? The mother of my daughter's friend? She found out she has breast cancer."

"Oh! I am so sorry to hear that," I'd said.

"Yeah. Well. But get this: She's just having a mastectomy. No chemotherapy, no radiation, nothing. It hasn't spread. That's it." She'd begun sobbing. "Why is it me? Why does it have to be me?"

"I don't know," I'd said. I'd kept rubbing her neck. How futile my hands looked.

After a little while we'd gone down the hall to the bathroom. She was off-balance, she'd lurched past the break room, where the secretaries with their coffees looked up, startled. I'd heard there'd been complaints about her using the toilet and sink.

In the bathroom, she took some pain pills, then went into a stall to use the toilet. While I was out of her sight, I'd washed my hands quietly, uncomfortable with the scent and feeling of her hair on my hands, and ashamed of my discomfort.

She'd come out and put lipstick on as I'd watched, leaning my hip against the sink. We were safe, for that moment. She closed her lipstick and announced, "Let's go out for lunch. I need the air, that's what I need, the fresh air."

Outside she'd said, "Oh! Feel that sun!" Like an old woman, she was grateful now for warmth. We'd walked slowly down the street, my arm through hers, holding her close. When we'd entered the restaurant, she shook me off. I crossed the room just ahead of her, watching out of the corner of my eye, afraid she would fall, and thinking with amazement of an ice skater's balance, able to twirl with her head thrown back.

My friend, reassured by our familiar surroundings, comforted by our lunch, talked on, clutching her tea mug, and as I listened to her voice and looked at her, released for a moment from her pain, I was plunged suddenly into my own. I understood, like a punch to the stomach, that this would be our last lunch here.

In her house, after feeding the little girls, I laid strips of bacon on mayonnaise, tomato, lettuce, and toast, and sliced our sandwiches carefully into four quarters. I arranged them on a plate with a piece of parsley, added our mugs of tea, put them on a tray and carried it all into her room. Her room was filled with the day's warmth. A fly was flinging itself against a windowpane. We ate in silence. When we were done, she asked, "Would you get my makeup bag out?"

Her daughter showed me where it was, and the two little girls followed me back into the room. Her daughter plumped up the pillows behind her mother's back. My daughter, silent, looked in turn at my friend and me. "Why don't you get out of bed?" she asked my friend, who didn't answer. She was holding a magnifying mirror to her face, trying to tweeze a hair. The little girls watched intently.

"Want me to do it?" I asked.

"Okay," she said. "I can't see the damn thing, I just feel it." I pulled out the hair.

I said, "You know, I have one in just the same spot. I guess we're just turning into little old ladies with whiskers on our chins." At once, I thought, *What a stupid thing to say*.

She put on mascara expertly. When she got out her lipstick, her daughter put her face up to her mother's—a small plant to its sun—and my friend put lipstick on her. Then, exhausted, she fell back against her pillows. I took the girls out.

When I returned, she said, "You know, I've been using that mascara for fifteen years, and now they've stopped making it?" She grimaced.

I said, "Want me to rub your neck?"

"Oh yes, please," she answered.

"Can you turn over?" I asked.

"Not really," she answered.

I lifted her to turn her over on her stomach. She smelled of freshly washed flannel. I rubbed her neck and looked over the bed out the window at the old barn, and the mountains.

"My friend whose husband died was here yesterday," she said, her voice muffled. "She said he would be waiting for me when I die, to help me. That made me feel good. I like to think of him being there for me."

"Mm-hmm," I said.

"That's what they say," she continued. "Kübler-Ross and those people? That when you die, there are people you know, your family or friends, to greet you or help you?"

"Mm-hmm," I said, "I remember reading that."

"Do you believe that?" she asked. "That what Kübler-Ross says is true? That people can come back? That it's possible to come back?"

"I don't know," I said. "Do you think it's possible?"

"I don't think she's crazy," she said.

I looked out the window at the mountains.

"I'm feeling better about the children," she said, after a while. She shifted her weight. "My daughter's had so much attention, I don't know if it's good for her. Her class talked about it with her at school. She told the class that her mommy was dying of cancer and they were very sympathetic."

I moved my hands up her neck, smoothing the downy hair. It's like she was on a boat, leaving shore, and all the rest of us were getting smaller and smaller to her.

My friend said, "You know what my daughter said to me? She said, 'If I kiss you a thousand times, will you still die?'"

I was afraid I would scream.

She was silent, and I slowly stopped rubbing her neck. As I was crossing to the door, she said, suddenly, "Wait!"

I turned back quickly, asked her, "What is it?"

"Could you kind of keep your eye on her, over the years, for me? It would make me feel better, knowing you said you would," she asked.

"Oh. Yes. Of course. I will," I said. I realized this was what I'd been waiting for.

That night, in my daughter's darkened room, the pink clown night-light glowing, I lay next to her and put my face in her neck, breathing in her grassy fragrance. Her thumb was in her mouth, her other hand stroking her blanket. She sucked loudly. Her thumb had a little yellow callus on it.

"I don't want to be a big woman, not for a long, long, time," she said.

"Why not?" I asked.

"Because when I'm really big, I'll be buried. When you're buried, you're all in the grass, and your head turns into a stone," she said.

I smoothed her heavy, satiny hair away from her forehead.

"Dead people climb on a ladder down into the ground and they are the grass and the flowers, and then they come alive again," she continued.

"I think," I said, "when people die, they leave their bodies and then they're different than we are."

She said, "You mean they disappear?"

"Sort of," I said.

"But where do they go? Do they live in the ground?" she asked.

"I don't know where they go." I said each word carefully, as if saying them that way would convince me. "I just think that God made us, and loves us, and when we die, we must be taken care of somehow."

My daughter was firm and confident: "When God made us, He stuck our skin on our blood and that's how we were made. Does God love me?" she asked.

"Oh, yes. Like Mommy loves you." I traced her silky eyebrows with my finger.

She was silent for a while. Then she asked, "Is it dark down there?"

From a Letter to My Mother

PART TWO

Oh, Mother. How lovely it would have been, to have you alive, and to have seen you get help, to have seen you come to understand what underwater currents were steering you. To have reclaimed that brilliant, joyous voice in your adolescent diaries. Could you have grown to acknowledge that my father could not see beyond his own needs? That you deserved so much more from him?

I want you to have lived longer because I want to think you would have been able to change. That you would have been able to get help—finally—and find relief from what my friend, after reading my book about you, *Missing*, called your "ancient loneliness," and your "broken-heartedness." I could have helped you. Healing, you could have sat down with me, in my husband's and my house, at our kitchen table, beneath the Buddha statue on our kitchen altar.

I would have made us a pot of tea. We would have gazed at one another—Mother! Daughter!—and smiled. We would have talked. You could have poured out your heart to me, Mother, and I would have carefully held all its broken pieces, without cutting myself on the shards. For I'm old enough, now. I'm seasoned. I have acquired a certain wisdom. I could take it. How sweet that would have been. To have reached that safe shore of healing.

We would have talked and talked. All that I would have asked you! To tell me about your father, who suddenly died when you were seven. Everything that you remember. How tall was he? Did we all get our terrible teeth from him? (Your mother had those amazing, white, even, strong teeth—she could have taken a bite out of any of us.) Did she talk to you about him? Wasn't it his sister who sent me presents from South Africa? What was she doing there? What happened to his brothers and sisters, to everyone?

43

I would have asked you why you loved my father. My friend said, after reading my book about you, that you seemed to love him so much. So much more than he deserved. That he was more important to you than your children. I told her I thought it was because you didn't know men. You'd lost your father, and your mother didn't remarry until you were grown. So you grew up without learning from a father what men can be like.

And the man you married—my father. As his old friend told me, he was "the handsomest man on campus." He was "wildly amusing, and like no one else." My friend who read my book, *Missing*, thought that having won him must have done a lot for your self-esteem. That all your life this helped you, knowing this man had chosen you. That you must have needed his love so much. Well, yes, I can imagine, Mother, because I didn't know what it felt like to be loved until my husband—my third!—loved me. But—I say this not to hurt you, Mother, but because it is true—my husband is capable of love, whereas my father was not: he, as I said, could not see past his own needs. Oh, I know, there's an explanation there, too. I could write a book about him, too—about his violent, alcoholic father, about his feelings of inadequacy. I could. But, as my friend says, "There's always an explanation, but that doesn't mean there's an excuse." My father sometimes hurt people. You didn't. At least, not on purpose.

I told my friend that, with a self-centered mother like yours, you'd been perfectly groomed for a self-centered husband. He stepped right into her shoes. As they say, it was "all about her," and then it was "all about him." And what about you? In your girlhood diary you wrote that your teacher said you "have a fine mind and know how to use it." What about that splendid intelligence? What about that enthusiasm, that wit? What about that girl who wrote in her diary, "I love life—and everything's beautiful!"

What about *her*?

I guess I'm going to have to bring out my therapeutic lightbox and sit in front of it for a few evenings to regulate my sleep.

This worked, last year, to re-set my internal clock so I could stop the cycle of getting sleepy early, then waking up in the wee hours. See, Mother? How I have learned that there can be solutions to problems?

It seems to me you were always tired. Of course, towards the end (your poor lungs), you had no stamina at all. You spent much of your day in the nursing home asleep. Or did you? I don't even know. I was a hundred-and-sixty-five miles away, in New Hampshire, a single mother with a job; I could only drive down to Massachusetts to visit you every few months.

I used to walk in my sleep, do you remember? As a child, and even as a young woman, I scared myself. What if I had walked into that lake I was living by, that first year of that first marriage? I was teaching, then, and I dreamt that my high school students were in our bedroom, cold, and I sleep-walked putting blankets out for them. When I woke the next morning, there were blankets in three places on the floor. If I could do that in my sleep, what was to prevent me from walking into the lake, dreaming I was swimming?

I think, now, I was afraid I would walk into the lake because I must have had an impulse to do so. To escape an intolerable situation. Deep-down I knew it was intolerable, but back then, I, too, was driven by underwater currents. I hadn't learned, yet, how to pay attention to my own needs, how to respect my intuitions. I had your (unfortunate) example before me — even if I was unaware I was following it — of not knowing what I felt, of putting the wrong people first. I learned from your example and the Church's hypocrisy — that priest you so admired, Mother, why did he have teenage boys living in his house? — that, in the words of that terrible prayer we said every Sunday, "Lord, I am not worthy to gather up the crumbs under Thy table," and that it was men whose needs and desires were to be fulfilled. We women were handmaidens of their will. You, brilliant woman that you were! You used to wash and iron that priest's vestments!

Emotions — especially anger — were not to be expressed, but rather to be repressed. I watched you swallow your anger.

I remember, as a child, sitting in the back seat of the car while you and my father were having some sort of altercation in the front seat. He was irritable and short with you, for some reason. I could see you were angry—a child knows her mother's face—and I saw your anger, and I saw you swallow it—I think you actually swallowed—and you let him talk to you like that. I remember thinking, "Oh! That's what I should do." A dangerous lesson. It took me so very long to unlearn it.

But the sleep problem, Mother. I remember you talking in your sleep, lying on the living room sofa. This was even before you were diagnosed with lung disease. You could be very amusing. You made puns in your sleep. I recall a long, witty sleep-talk punning on the word "purr." You said, "What does a hip cat poet like? Purr-verse."

Why were you so often napping? I guess because, by then, the energy you must have expended raising five children—cooking all those meals, washing all those clothes—had left you. I was the last child at home, and you'd settled into a permanent depression. You were tired all the time (your poor lungs).

Mother, I've often dreamt of you. Sometimes, you appear and I realize, with a feeling of betrayal and disbelief, that you have not been dead at all. You've been alive, all these years, and I didn't know it. But if you were alive, why didn't you come to see me? I don't understand. And I can't get you to look at me. Just like in real life. To this day, I feel hurt, invisible, if someone important to me looks away when I am talking to him or her. So in the dream, as in life (when you were alive) I'm seeking your eyes. Those lovely hazel almond-shaped eyes. (Your granddaughter has them. Your grandson, too. Only theirs are blue.)

Sometimes, during the years I was writing my book, *Missing*, about you, I dreamt that you appeared and I would have the chance to ask you all the questions that remain unanswered. But as I approached, you'd disappear. I'd realize—again—that I'd never, never know some things. There was so much that I'd never, ever, be able to find out.

I've had the same kind of dream about your mother—my grandmother: a dream that I've found her. She's not dead, and I've found her, and she'll tell me everything I'm dying (living) to know. But, of course, it comes to naught, that dream. The feeling of terrific excitement mounts, and then abruptly is aborted. She is silent. She's alive, in my dream, but silent. I'll never, never find out. I'll never ever know.

From some of my dreams of you I would wake crying. I cry easily. Perhaps I cry so much because you cried so little. I am shedding your tears, too, as I carry your grief, as well as my own. I don't want to die of unshed tears, as I believe you did. What else is drinking, smoking, and taking drugs? It's all about swallowing feelings. As I remember you doing, from fifty years ago. Swallowing anger. Swallowing grief. Never letting it out. Never ever letting it out.

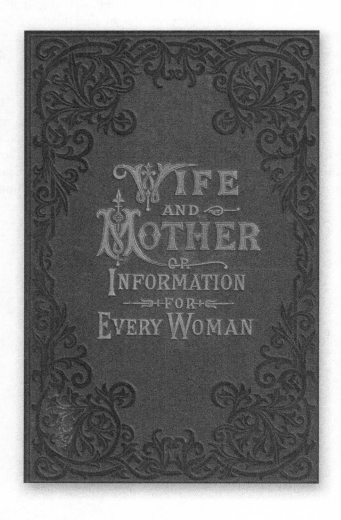

Episode 6

Three Husbands

FROM MY DIARY:

At home in Illinois, my daughter, now five, is playing in my jewelry box. In it are two wedding rings: a heavy, wide gold ring from my brief marriage to my son's father; and a thin, beveled gold band from my marriage to my daughter's father. I am wearing the third, a rounded, antique gold band, for I am married, now, to the man I met at the writers' conference. My daughter says, "I'm gonna be like you and have three husbands when I grow up."

"Oh! No, it's better to have just one," I reply. "If you can be happy."

A big day: kindergarten for my daughter. And for my son, just turned fourteen, his freshman year of high school. We are up at 7 a.m. with an order to follow: breakfast, packing lunches, showers and getting dressed and out the door, or tardy bells. I drive my son to the high school, and then my husband and I walk my daughter the few blocks to our neighborhood elementary school.

A perfect first-day-of-school day, cool and crisp. The children are flocking like little birds to the schoolyard where teachers are carrying signs with their names on them. Parents are milling around, looking both proud and anxious. One mother blows a cloud of blue cigarette smoke upward into the sunny air.

My daughter's back is straight, expectant. She's holding her pink Care Bear bag with gym shoes, lunch, Crayola markers and milk money inside. A child runs crying after his mother, who turns to hug him one last time.

⌣

My fortieth birthday. I heard a young mother say to her little girl at a bus stop I was walking by, "I just couldn't wait to get home to see you!" and realized that I never heard that sentiment when I was a child, from my mother, or from anyone, until my (third) husband. That I've had this giant hole in me, not even knowing it was there.

⌣

School for me, too: I'm in Social Work Graduate School, and that, and the children, and the house, take up 95 percent of my time, though my husband shares all the housework and cooking and is able to be home after school on days when I cannot. Today, when I don't have classes or field work, I wash dishes, take my husband to work, call the pediatrician's office, pick up medicine for my skin at the pharmacy, go to the bank and the office supply store, take my daughter to a friend's, and then study. Then I get my daughter, my husband and son come home, we make dinner, do dishes, maybe watch a TV show. I make a bath for my daughter in the old porcelain claw-footed tub — my daughter and I had painted the claws with red nail polish — then I or my husband read to her before bed. I study more. These days of going, going, going. I itch for more time, more peace, but, for whatever, reason, I itch on my abdomen.

There is the crumbling foundation of our old house that

needs to be fixed; a report due for fieldwork; the money to be collected for a co-worker's going-away gift; the plans and hotel reservation for a social work conference; there are the unwritten letters; a long-overdue wedding gift for a friend; a bike lock for my son; a book to be picked up at the library; my daughter's ice-skating audition schedule; my son's soccer; friends for Sunday-night dinner; the cat box; the haircut appointment; more school clothes; the check for the Special Olympics. I want to keep writing, but I wonder when I can. If I rise early, this fall, I can at least write here in my diary, which I've neglected.

Such a beautiful morning. My husband filled the apricot-colored wooden bowl with limes, peaches, nectarines, apples, bananas. "Look at this! Take a picture of this, will you!" he said exuberantly. We woke to two fragrant little girls in their night-gowns playing in my daughter's room; her friend has spent the night. And two heavily-sleeping adolescent boys, my son and a friend on the TV room pull-out couch, brownie crumbs from a late-night cooking spree by the boys trailing from the pan, through the kitchen, to the TV room. My son took a shower after midnight, his third of the day, and woke my husband.

I dream I have to have an operation and I'm not sure there will be anesthesia. Maybe it's because we drove the children, for spring vacation, to their father's in New Hampshire that I find myself full of old, gloomy memories, thinking a lot about the years past, of my youth gone, of my young body, and the overwhelming number of unhappy memories I have of those years.

It is the very young and optimistic face of a waitress in a diner in this lakeside town we're passing through on our way back that brings those thoughts to me. I should know that youth does not guarantee contentment—rarely contentment; at the best, brief happiness, or perhaps it is the optimism of youth that I wish for, the sense that you have your whole life in front of you. By the time I was twenty-one I was married for the first time, and even before then my youth was, in truth, not very happy. So it is someone else's youth I long for.

⌣

A happy day with my daughter. No deadlines or rushing from one place to another. We have lunch and I buy her clothes, and we look in my favorite second-hand store at round dining tables. I would really like to have one for Thanksgiving. The hairdresser cutting my daughter's bangs tells her, "When I have a little girl, I want her to look just like you!"

My daughter's little friend is here today. In the pocket of her coat is a note from her mother saying "Don't ever give her to her father or his wife!" On the way home from school, she and my daughter are holding hands and we're talking about the classroom open house that night. I tell my daughter that I will go and she will stay home with her stepfather. My daughter asks if her friend will stay home with her father, and her friend says, "I don't have a dad."

My daughter asks softly, "Why not? Did he die?"

Her friend replies, "No! It was a long, long, time ago, before I even remember."

Then she puts her hand over her mouth and whispers through her fingers, "He was stolen away by a wicked stepmother!"

My daughter, horrified, says, "So she took him?"

"Yup. And then she married him!" says her friend.

My daughter asks, "Did he love her?"

Her friend replies scornfully, "Nah!"

My daughter says, "Why don't you live with your father and stepmother?"

Her friend replies, "Because they're BAD!"

They run ahead of me on the sidewalk.

⌣

Me to my teenage son, by way of some explanation for some restriction: "There are so many things you're just completely unaware of!"

He replies, "Like what?" and then realizes what he's said and we laugh.

Then he says to me, "Well, there are so many things that you are unaware of!"

And I say, not to be funny, and not realizing, either, what I am saying, "Well, like what?" and then we laugh again.

⌣

Summer is here and the children have left for New Hampshire for four weeks. It is as if a loud noise has suddenly stopped. My husband and I have been running a race during the past school year—running through each week, barely on top of his job and my school, our new family's life—to the weekends, when we collapsed, panting, until Monday. But now that's over. The children have departed for their father's, leaving me, their first and only mother, and my husband, who married the three of us (the four of us, really, counting my ex-husband), in this silence.

I waited for this moment, sometimes prayed for it, but now that it's come, I feel lost, sad, and suddenly unanchored. Back from the airport, I go first to my son's room, not only to see what he's left on—the fan, a radio, four lights—but what he has left behind that will make me miss him already. The debris of his adolescence, which irritates me in the midst of the school year, touches me in his absence, and I pick up his yearbook, a note in his handwriting, even his t-shirt, which I hold to my face. My daughter's room is more than I can confront, just yet, and I simply close the door, because her room, still, is full of what she calls her "stuffed-up animals," and the cord between us feels too short to stretch all the way to the East Coast.

⌣

I hate two households, as much, I think, as they do. I sat holding back tears in the airport terminal as the big plane pulled away, wishing it had been in my power to provide them with one happy household, one father, no summer absences. My daughter quieted in the last few days before departure and petted the cats incessantly. My son—as tall as me, now—looked strained.

Their father came a month ago for my daughter's piano recital. Sitting at the recital in a row with these three male persons—my husband, my ex-husband, my son—I feel my responsibility as the one whose body connects us all to try to knit up the spaces among us, though it seems impossible. As we all walked back to the car after the recital, I pulled out my camera to take a photograph. Farthest ahead is my ex-husband, his back to me, already nearly out of the frame; my husband, turning to look at me, waits for me; the children walk together. They know that they, at least, belong together; if they were to walk with a father, which would it be, and how would the other one feel?

Recently my girlhood friend was visiting. It seemed that everything in her life matched: her Chanel purse and makeup bag, her children and their father. She said she'd gotten everything she ever wanted, and her worst moment, she said, was when her goldfish jumped out of the bowl and died on the floor. But she's joking. Or is she? She wonders why she isn't satisfied. She thinks her small children are "too secure" and need some challenges. She says she tells them "I'll give you to the gypsies!" if they misbehave. Hearing this, I'm no longer envious. Maybe two households are not the worst thing.

Episode 7

Ellison Bay

FROM MY DIARY:

Now that I have a regular salary from my first social work job, at a hospital mental health center, we've bought a little cottage in Ellison Bay, Wisconsin, a four-and-a-half-hour drive from our home. My great-great-grandfather was one of Wisconsin's first cheese-makers, and renowned for having said, "I always speak to a cow as I would to a lady." Later, his son, my great-grandfather, in Iowa, had a cheese factory, so maybe some molecules of me remember Wisconsin, remember the farm. I'm half a Midwesterner, half a New Englander. This part of Wisconsin, the Door County peninsula, is said to be a little like Cape Cod, but it's not, really. Where is home? I miss New England. I miss New Hampshire. Where would I be buried, when I don't know where home is?

At a second-hand store near Ellison Bay, I found a 1950 calendar, one of those calendars businesses used to give away at Christmas. The sentimental illustration, titled "The End of a Perfect Day," shows a sunset beyond the fields of a farm, the farmer on his tractor being greeted by his wife, in a white apron, at the open gate to the field; by his daughter, a doll hanging from her hand; by his son, holding the gate open; and, yes, even by a collie dog, tail wagging. I tacked it to the kitchen wall of the cottage so I can pretend such an intact, happy family, in such a place, exists. Idyllic farm days in 1950 Wisconsin.

Never mind the other side of rural life, the black deeds, the suicidal wife, the crazy neighbor who kept a child in the attic; here in the village we heard the story of an old neighbor man, who, when his wife said that their dog shed hair all over their house, got up from his chair, not saying a word, took the dog out the back door, and shot it.

⌒

I'm feeling young, alone with my husband this last weekend in Ellison Bay before the children return from their father's. There is a time on the long drive up when I finally feel relaxed, and take a big deep breath—the "cleansing breath" they called it in childbirth classes. The road stretches out ahead of us. The air is cool, crisp, yet warm in the sun. The farms lie on both sides of the road, and on the east, beyond the farms, there's the cerulean blue of the lake. I'm able to leave the cares and worries of my other life behind me.

Once we are on the peninsula, the light by now is pink from the low sun, out of sight beyond the trees. The air is northern, with its hint of chill, and the hills and barns to the west become bathed in the soft pink light. A short drive, then, through a wooded area, where the tall trees make a canopy over the road.

For the first time we stop at The Top Deck, a supper club on the North Bay. Just as they advertised, there is a beautiful twilight here, too, on the opposite side of the peninsula, a pearly mauve and turquoise sunset in the water. The one-man-band plays trumpet, organ, and banjo, while beating his bass drum with one foot and his rigged-up snare drum with the other. We listen, and gaze out at the long black pier and two solitary ducks, also black, gently riding tiny waves. Big spiders, spinning their webs all along the outside edge of the roof, are silhouetted in black against the pearly glow. We dance, my husband's hands and body warm, familiar and stirring at the same time.

Then, to this home, our cottage, what was once a fishing club, sledded long ago across Green Bay from the Upper Peninsula on deep winter ice, and put down in this spot near the little village. We will wake to birdsong, and the rhythms of this place once lived in by those who fished and cut timber.

Episode 8

I Would Like to Be an Egg

I was visiting in New Hampshire again, and went to see my best friend's daughter, who was now eight, and her brother, four. I was struck at once by the echoes of my friend's face in theirs; but also by her son's continually puzzled and distraught look.

But her daughter's long, dark hair, the hair that my best friend had taken such pride in, that had never been cut since the child's birth—that hair has been shorn by her father's new girlfriend. Gone is that long hair for which I had brought ivory plastic barrettes. But how sweet she looked, how like her mother when her hair was growing back after chemotherapy.

Her father, with his children in the car, picked me up from where I was staying and drove us to their house, that century-old farm set in the flinty New Hampshire earth. From the back seat, my friend's eight-year-old daughter asked how her mother and I met, and I told her how we had both been helping a social service agency and how people had said we looked alike, and then we'd learned we were born one day apart.

Her four-year-old brother suddenly shouted, "My Mommy's dead!"

"I know she is," I replied gently.

When we arrived at the farm, the children took me to see their neighbor's horse with its new foal, which was nuzzling the mother's teat. The mare leaked milk onto the foal's small hoof, and I thought of my own milk when I had my two babies, and of my best friend nursing her daughter, then her son; of the pain she got in her breast when nursing him and then of that diagnosis of breast cancer.

Inside the house, her son was full of comments about bad boys and girls, and worries about bad things happening. His sister gave me a headband she'd made in camp. "I was going to give it to her" (her father's girlfriend), she said, "but when I heard you were here I decided to give it to you." It's a little too small for me, but I wear it anyway.

I said, "I have presents for you both, too, in my present bag." My friend's son said, "I love presents!"

His sister and I smiled a lot at each other. He opened his present and smiled at the crayons and the sharpener, and his sister said, precisely like a mother, "You have to hold it up like this, or the stuff gets out. I had one like this."

She opened the book I brought her, then the cream-colored plastic barrettes. She voiced an "Ooh!" of pleasure, though they weren't going to work in short hair. Her brother began to use his crayons, but his father wanted him to come outside for a photo, so we all trooped out. But the little boy cried and threatened to break up all the crayons and rip up the paper.

He'd said, earlier, in the car, "Daddy, why when I say something then you say something right after and I don't get to finish saying it?" and muttered threats about how he'd tear something up "if . . ." and his father had told him, "Just say 'Excuse me but I wasn't finished talking.'"

But now, his father commanded, "Put your head up and smile!" and counted, "One, two, three!" Up came his little son's head; he was scowling, crying, he rubbed his fists in his eyes, but he posed for the photo. I patted his small, tense back.

Back inside, drawing, he said he "can't do it right!" and nearly cried when his paper slipped to the floor. His father sent him upstairs until he could "act nicely." He returned, after a few moments.

I asked to help him draw and he liked that. He drew a rainbow, and seven perfect stars. He signed his name, the letters all backward, and showed it to us, saying, "I drew this picture for all of you, so no one will be mean to me anymore."

I sat next to him at dinner, which was "volcano" eggs (soft poached). He was going to show me the "volcano eruption" as he plunged his fork in, but the eggs were too hard and it didn't work, and he cried. His father said he'd make more eggs, and his son calmed down. During the meal, the boy pointed out that I forgot to put the cap on the salad dressing, and I said, "You're right, I did, sometimes grown-ups don't do things right, like kids, huh?"

His father and I talked politely, the children vying for my attention, me taking the little boy's hand whenever I could, gazing into his blue eyes, so like his mother's, and his many perfect teeth. He only had four when last I saw him.

After dinner his father sent them to put on pajamas, but the little boy wandered, lost, across the floor. "I want someone to help me!" he said.

"May I?" I asked. He said yes.

He and his sister and I went up the stairs, and she took us into her room. "What a beautiful room!" I said. She showed me her school certificate and the poster of a book on her wall. Her brother reached toward two large framed pictures of their mother on the bookshelf.

He said, "Mommy! I want her! I want Mommy!"

"I know you do," I said.

While his sister put her pajamas on, he and I went to his room where he zoomed a flashing truck for me. When he pulled open a drawer to get his pajamas, the dresser began to tip, and my exclamation, "Watch out!" frightened him. This four-year-old was used to being frightened by catastrophe—no, not used to it. But simply poised for one at any time. "It's okay, it's okay," I reassured him.

I carried his pajamas and on the way downstairs he pointed to a photo on the wall—his father's girlfriend, who lived here but was not yet home from work. "They say they're in love!" he told me.

"What do you think?" I asked.

"I say they're not!" he replied. "If they were, I would have come out of her tummy." Then he led me, triumphantly, to the girlfriend, herself, who had just arrived. I said how nice it was to meet her, although, considering the little girl's shorn hair, I was worried. I began to help my friend's little son into his pajamas, but he wanted the girlfriend to do it.

As his sister came back down the stairs, I was standing in the kitchen next to her father's girlfriend, my arm around her shoulder. My friend's daughter made a place for herself between us, and said, "Here are my two most favorite ladies in the world, except there is one who is not here."

It was bedtime. I asked to go upstairs with her, and we did, and I sat on her bed and she talked about bedtimes, and the bad dreams she had, and how she hates the bad dreams when they seem "really real." I hugged her and said goodnight.

I went to her brother's room. When I said his bed was very cozy, he said, "I would like to be an egg. Inside an egg."

"Wouldn't that be great?" I said. "All cozy and warm."

"What do chickens think when they're inside a shell?" he wondered.

"They don't think like us," I said, "they don't worry about anything."

"But the egg would crack and break!" he said.

"Maybe not," I said, "if it has a strong shell."

"If the heavy rain and snow came, it would crack," he said.

I said, "No, it's very strong. Nothing would crack. You'd be safe and warm and cozy in it."

"Would you be in it, too?" he asked.

"Wouldn't that be fun? We'd visit with each other," I said.

"I want to visit you at your house," he said.

"I want you to," I said. But I knew how unlikely it was, because of the distance between Illinois and New Hampshire, and also, I could tell the girlfriend did not like me, because I had been their mother's friend.

My friend's little boy explained how his bed used to be in a different place in his room. "That's when you didn't know me," he said. Of course he didn't remember that I did know him, that I used to hold him, that I spent so much time with him and his sister and their mother; of course he didn't remember that very last afternoon I'd spent here with them, not long before his mother died.

I kissed him goodnight, but on my way to the downstairs I heard a sound from his sister's room and so I went in. She sat up suddenly and I saw she was crying. I bent over her and she said, "I know what it is about you—you are like my Mommy," and she threw her arms around me. I cried a little too, and held her. I felt as if my arms were her mother's arms.

"I miss your mother, too," I said.

"You are half my Mommy, you are two-thirds my Mommy, I think!" she sobbed.

I said, "I loved your mother and I love you. Your mother specially asked me to be your friend. And I hope we can see each other and I can tell you all about your mother, and what she was like." I said this, though I knew I probably could not make it happen.

"Why do people have to die?" she asked me. "Especially people you love?"

"I don't know," I said, stroking her short hair. "I only know that we feel so sad, and then that feeling can get better, after a while, and we can also feel happy again. Your mother can't come back, but there are other people for you to love. None of them are her, or can be her, but you can love them, and they can love you."

"You mean I have a happy part, and a sad part?" she asked. "Like the top half of me is happy, and the bottom half is sad? And I could just cut off the sad part?"

"We can't cut off the sad part, but we all have those sad and those happy parts," I said, "all of those parts are in you and in me and in everyone." We rocked a little, and hugged. I told her how happy her mother was with her, how proud she was of her, and how she used to bring her to my house when she was a baby and nurse her.

"Do you feel better now?" I asked.

"Uh huh. You can go downstairs, now, if you want. I can go to sleep," she said.

"I will see you again," I said.

But it would be many years before I did.

Episode 9

The Land of Change

The stuffed clown flew across my social work office and hit me in the head. "Use words," I said to the six-year-old girl. "Use words to tell me if you're mad, don't throw the clown." Part of my work as a therapist was to help people learn the power of their own words.

Listening to their words and using my own to show I heard and understood them, I was sometimes witness and midwife to the slow, painful rebirth of people whom language had failed.

A week later the six-year-old was carefully cutting paper. "This," she announced, pointing to a rectangular hole she had made in a piece of paper "is a door to the land of change." Not only our words, but others' words, too, can be that door to the land of change. Having our feelings acknowledged, listened to, and respected, perhaps for the first time, helps us integrate and regulate our emotions and our actions. Someone tells what has happened to her, and by being listened to, begins to be able to see it differently. "I didn't know I could free myself with my words," one woman said to me.

For some, words have been used mostly to wound. I think here of a woman whose mother had called her, when she was a child, "The Thing." Speaking of this as a grown woman, many years later, she wore a slight smile. Part of our work together was to free her from that smile, to allow herself to feel for the first time her grief and rage. Her recovery could not begin without seeing the reality of her mother's cruelty. If we do not want to pass on to others the unexpressed pain we ourselves have experienced, we must find it, feel it, name it, and talk about it.

I think of a mother who was able to cry when she told me of having been locked in her room, hungry, looking at pictures of food in a magazine. Because she was able to recall and feel her own pain, she would not pass on such torment to her own two children, and was eager to be a loving mother to them.

When I was working at a community mental health center, a woman was assigned to me (and to the psychiatrist, for medication evaluation) who was "developmentally delayed," according to her thick pile of evaluations from various hospitals, clinics, and schools. In addition, she had been born with severe physical disabilities that made her conspicuous. The simplest tasks of life were difficult for her and people often stared and even ridiculed her. Severely depressed, she had several times tried to kill herself.

Every week for a year-and-a-half, she braved the city trains and buses to come to my office in the mental health center and sit with me. Usually she spoke only a few sentences, maybe one paragraph in all, and sometimes said nothing for the entire session.

Having surmised that some people were silent because they'd never had anyone who wanted to listen to them, I tried to meet her silence with cheerful invention. I asked questions, and answered them myself, as though she were on the other end of a phone. I would guess at her answers, and confirm the rightness of my guess by her smallest show of feeling. Or we might sit together in silence.

Sometimes I would sing, or read to her. I felt, from her eyes, which were very alive in her otherwise frozen face, that however simple these times together were, she was finding something of value in them, and her repeated, long and difficult journeys gave me reason to hope it was so. It felt like I was holding the warmth of a human presence up to her so that she could melt.

Trying to explain to her why we needed to communicate with each other, I drew a picture of us together, with arrows for words from my mouth to her ears, and from her mouth to my ears. I drew colors inside us to represent our feelings, which we could communicate to each other with words, but which stayed imprisoned inside us if we didn't speak.

When I drew us as two identical female figures, her tears fell. They fell off her cheeks and into her lap, and she didn't wipe them from her face—as though these were her first, and she didn't know what to do with them.

At the end of our last session—I was leaving the agency—she left me a letter. She had written six flowing pages, in beautiful handwriting. Her sentences were those of a person acutely aware of her own pain and isolation, who needed to be close to others. I saw from the letter that indeed she had been listening, and that now with her own words she could tell me what she had been thinking and feeling all those months—tell me rather than have me continue to guess. She had never been—might never be—able to speak of her feelings, fears, and wishes, but she could write them in sentences that were direct, clear, and full of feeling. Her words had acquired a value previously unknown, for they had succeeded in making her known to another.

IA 6833 N

7/23/09

Episode 10

The Blue Hours

My daughter's friend slept over last night. I overheard the nine-year-old girls, swearing friendship "till death us do part," and at that moment, remembered placing my cheek on my best friend's cheek when I said goodbye and moved away to be with my new husband.

It had been painful to divorce, to give up that dream of a happy family, but in a deeper way, perhaps because marriage is so complicated and friendship is usually simpler, it was more painful to leave my friend. She lived about one month more.

⌣

My daughter is back again from her father's in New Hampshire. We drove up to Ellison Bay late last night, with her crying "I want my Daddy!" and hugging in one arm the bear he gave her. It is hard to see her sad, to just be with her sadness, but after I got in the back seat with her, and she had both cats in one arm, she chattered, nonstop, and then abruptly fell asleep and slept for the rest of the drive.

It was wonderful arriving in the black night: a new view of the peninsula, with the moon hanging huge and very yellow over the orchards and farms. It's good to have our girl back. Today is for our recuperation. Like mother cats we will be sniffing and reclaiming our kitten.

⌣

My moods change so, but my sadness persists. "Dysphoria" is the official psychological term for "a profound state" of sadness and unease. "I can't stand the way I look!" I say to myself, looking into the car mirror, but my daughter is there and hears me; I need to watch what I say. Do I really think I must look, be, beautiful? That I'm not worthy of notice unless I am beautiful? I recall advice about a woman's appearance that was so common when I was growing up—a book about charm, with chapters on how to dress, what expression you should have on your face, your posture, the tone of your voice, how to take off a coat! Oh, and how to be graceful, when you should and shouldn't laugh, advice about your skin, your hair, your make-up, your perfume, and how always, always to be aware of the eye of the beholder.

Helena Rubinstein, one of the women who began the cosmetic industry, even actually said that for women, "Beauty is a duty." In nine years when my daughter is eighteen and I'm fifty-one, she'll have youth and beauty, and I hope my days of looking in the mirror too often will be over. A woman dare not, at any age, be dependent on her looks for self-worth, but girls are so vulnerable to it. My daughter said of her father's new wife, who has had a baby, "She looks more like a mom, now, kind of friendly and tired-out; still pretty but in a different way." And she comments on how I look like the "At-Home Mom" sometimes and other times the "Going-To-Work Mom." She likes the At-Home Mom best.

Beauty aside, on what can one rely for self-esteem, for feelings of usefulness and worth? A basic conviction not only that one is lovable, but also that one is capable of loving.

My son leaves tomorrow for college. When I am scouring the closet looking for towels for him to take, I suddenly realize "He's leaving," and I go downstairs to say it to him. He is feeling it, too, and we embrace and both cry a little. He's trembling, and sweaty, his young body heat twice my middle-aged one, burning much hotter. We just hold on to each other for a few minutes.

This is my son's eighteenth birthday and I cannot sleep. It did not feel good to talk to him on the phone from college. His voice sounds different. He sounds free. I didn't know that his leaving meant he would be placing himself outside our whole context, that the break would be so big. I wake on this morning of his eighteenth birthday to a dream of trying, vainly, to reattach him, as he is today, to an umbilical cord, which is too long and too thin; is no longer necessary; is, in fact, ridiculous. I feel old and tired. My daughter said of my comment about him sounding free: "It's like he was in a forest, before, and now he's out in the open." Then she put her head on my shoulder—for now, she still wants to stay in the forest, and I'm grateful.

In Ellison Bay again, and our friend, on a road trip to see his old mother in North Dakota, has stopped to stay with us one night. It adds to our pleasure of being here. He's napping on a lawn chair under a cotton blanket inside our backyard's blue screen-tent. Last night we were listening to him talk about his little son's death many years ago. He said that he couldn't—can't—believe that life itself is bad or unjust, because so many people have loved him, beginning with his mother. I wish that I could have had that certainty of being loved. But his grief rose up, still, and he said, "I don't think I can talk about this anymore."

It's overcast and cold. Our friend left very early. I could feel his heavy tread shaking our whole small cottage. We had talked more about his grief over his child and my depression. I said it seems his feeling was pure, a pure sadness, whereas this depression is confusing, full of self-dislike, regret, and is frightening and unintelligible to others, like my husband, who does not understand it. I can talk about it to my psychiatrist, who is prescribing anti-depressants, but not really to my husband. I didn't say all that—I wanted to—but our friend moved me when he recited a poem from memory, and I could hardly speak at all.

I feel left out when he and my husband speak of their books and share their work, but I remember reading, in that useful book about depression, that your worth is not dependent on what you do. But I don't know if worth is the issue, or the feeling that I haven't written what I hoped to. After all, we three met at the writers' conference, but as yet I have little to show for it. Our friend has a wonderful, old beat-up briefcase to hold his work. I brought mine in a loose pile. Maybe diary-writing is my main writing work.

My other work, as a therapist, is partly to listen. One of my social-work clients said to me, when I asked her what she had hoped for in her marriage, "Somebody to listen." There is a kind of beauty in my work at times that makes me believe it's worthwhile. It's as if I'm holding my warmth close to someone else—as I was with the woman who couldn't speak—and helping them to melt the pain that has caused them to freeze inside.

I especially like working with children. Beautiful in their approach to life, and touching when they are in pain, I see how often children are not helped, although it is not hard to help them. If it doesn't happen, it is usually because their parents were in so much pain themselves. Yet help goes so very far with children.

I am thinking of a seven-year-old child I counseled. He had been abused as a toddler, and in his first years with his kind foster parents would duck when someone approached his bed. His foster parents and I hoped that their care, and his and my steady, peaceful sessions of play therapy, could weave a fabric of trust that would sustain him.

Just before Christmas, he brought some candies with him to our appointment, which he dealt out, like cards, evenly between us. I noticed he kept the only chocolate candy for himself, and understood that the chocolate was especially precious to this child for whom so much had not been provided.

During our play session, he had braided together the tails of two plastic horses—"Like us," he had said, and moved closer to me on the rug where we sat. When it was time to go, he stopped before opening the door, to turn off the overhead light in order to admire the colored Christmas lights I had draped on my large green plant. Standing at the door to look back at the "tree," he suddenly returned to it to lay beneath its branches his chocolate candy.

Today I will take a vigorous walk for the sake of my neurotransmitters. Tonight I will take my little orange pills, and go to sleep. Sometimes it feels as though all I have added to a day is my own weight. As if the whole world is alive except me.

The pace of life in Ellison Bay is so different from the city; orderly and unhurried. Part of it is simply feeling safe, physically, not worried about locks, or where other people are; a relaxed and comfortable unity between inside and outside, much more connection to the natural world and its pleasures: the sound of leaves when the breeze quickens, the sounds of birds, the odor of the air itself, and of blossoms, the warmth of the sun. I imagine twelve months of it could be tedious, but for me, now, it's like water for a great thirst.

A few hours after I fell asleep last night, I dreamt that I had a bird's-eye view of earth, that I was in a kind of heaven that was awesomely beautiful and peaceful. I realized the people below me, the mortals, didn't need to be so worried about everything, including death, because this was the beautiful place they would be going to, and they would understand everything.

⸺

I'm in the blue screen-tent. A new bird I haven't heard before is singing what sounds like Peabody! Peabody! I'm drinking my morning coffee in here. The cats are in the upstairs windows like bookends. Last night we went to the movie theater in Baileys Harbor, a damp, metal building, musty, smelling like a child's rubber boots. The movie was Harrison Ford in one of his adventure films, like a cartoon, except for the number of deaths and the amount of blood. It was odd to come out of the theater and find ourselves in Baileys Harbor, the lake still and dark blue across the street. A very bright star was overhead. Driving home, my husband said he felt a little scared of how empty the place was: "Where is everybody?" I was happy to hear him admit such a mood because sometimes it seems I'm alone with my anxieties. While one of the pleasures of being here is feeling safe, because there isn't that city-tension constantly with you, the distance between people, as my husband put it, on some roads and in the countryside, can feel too great. At home, if you yelled, a neighbor would hear you shout but not on this road. We felt even a little homesick driving back to our cottage through the dark empty country.

Then we went, shortly, to bed. The cats were unhappy in the room with the water heater, so I let them out. I heard a big thunk as I was falling asleep, and this morning I found that heavy glass jug I'd bought at a secondhand store, unbroken, on the floor. Chasing after bugs, the cats had been leaping wildly around and knocked it over.

I had a quiet day, writing, so that at four p.m. yesterday I felt suddenly sick of the quiet and slow pace and we went out. I got a letter from my daughter at camp. She has made me a brace-let. "I hope you like it, Mom," she wrote, and told of her being allowed by her counselor to spot the water skiers. And though there's "I'm having a great time here at camp," still there's also "I miss you very much," and "I'm making new friends but I miss the old ones." Her letter ended with "I love you," and in cursive writing her full name and middle initial.

It's an intense pleasure to get mail here. I go across the road with quickened pulse to the little, white-frame, one-story post office, and stand at the small counter. I ask the very round post-mistress—she looks like Mrs. Tiggy-winkle in the Beatrix Potter book—if we have any mail. She'll glance at me and say, "Noth-ing today," if we don't, but if we do, she turns toward the corner where they hold general delivery mail and I feel as if there's been a tug on a fishing line. No friendly small talk from her, though. We are from "Away," as people say up here about those of us who are not natives, and especially those of us from Illi-nois. So far, we've had two letters from my daughter, and have written her every day, so I hope she is also getting pleasure from receiving mail.

I'm sitting in a folding chair in the little room where the small wrapped-in-insulation water heater is. I've just painted the walls white, and am in the midst of a mess of paint brushes and news-paper and rags on the floor. I decided to fix up this room and use it as a study because it has two windows, the most light, and I can hear the birdsongs. I'm up early to get the most enjoyment out of the day. Both cats followed me in and the boy-cat leaps up on top of the small water heater and purrs. The girl-cat sits neatly on the seat of the stool under the window. She has wrap-ped her tail around her feet and watches the morning.

From the north window in this room, I see only low branch-es of spruce, and, at this hour, sunlight splashing through them as if someone had thrown a bucket of light. The mourning dove calls. Robins are loud, "the optimists of birds," I told my husband.

The feeling in this room is just what I hoped it would be: peaceful, reflective, and close to the outdoors.

The boy-cat is lying down now, asleep atop the warm water heater. Both cats still show evidence of their traumatic kittenhood before they were rescued by the shelter, where I found them. The girl-cat has achieved some serenity. The boy-cat is anxious when I leave the room and he follows me. In my depressed hours, it is a comfort when the boy-cat seeks me out, comes close to me, and, almost like a friend, reaches out an orange-and-white front paw to touch me.

My daughter is with us up here now. She still smells like her child-self, her neck like a kind of fruity hard apricot, but her whole suntanned self looks like a pre-teen, now, not like a little girl. While I am declining, she is maturing and ripening.

I woke early in our bed apart from my husband, feeling the effects of our quarrel. My skin feels a sort of itch to be touched. In normal life, we swim like fish in and out of each other's space. I lay there thinking of getting up without touch and of the long hours until bedtime and of the waste of time and comfort it is to be in our war. So I moved next to him. What is won? What is lost? Life flows on. It is like water.

And though I cleaned the cottage and took my daughter out to lunch and to get a video, I have cabin fever; then my ex-husband called from New Hampshire, a quick, hostile exchange, resulting in my tears and trembling as I hung up the phone. My daughter comes in to say, "So you're mad at both your husbands?"

I dreamt I was in some battle that nobody would count as a war, but one could be killed nonetheless.

And my husband told me he dreamt I had a bad twin who would kill me. He was very worried about me, running around trying to save my life. People were trying to convince him the good twin had never existed, but he had proof of it, witnesses of the life we've had together. I think the bad twin is this depression of mine.

⌒

In the winter, back at home, in our warm living room with its thick, deep-green rug that conceals the whole beat-up pine floor, so green that it might be a grassy clearing in a forest, and in front of the decorated Christmas tree, I'm reading in the newspaper about Romania. My daughter is holding the boy-cat, who stretches a soft, furry paw to pat her face.

I read that soldiers in a forest in Romania ripped open the belly of a pregnant woman. My daughter is chattering to me, and the cat is blinking at the tree lights, at the pile of shining gifts. Also in that story, in Timisoara, Romania, a woman doctor bathed patients with water and her bare hands, because soap and washcloths were unavailable. Although usually I only write in the morning, I get my diary so I can write that down. My daughter and I are here, and not in the forest, but some other mother could be, and some other daughter.

"Are you writing in your diary?" my daughter asks.

"Yes," I answer. "I'm writing about how terrible and wonderful people are." I tell her, not about the pregnant woman but of soldiers killing people, and the doctor's hands. She strokes the cat's silky fur.

"Why do the soldiers kill people?" she asks.

I answer, "Because they're cruel, because they hate." She's quiet for a moment.

"Just like the girls at school," she says. "Let's be mean to her!" those girls decided, when she said something they didn't like. They wrote her a letter, telling her they hated her, and put it into her school locker. She cried and cried two nights ago from this.

81

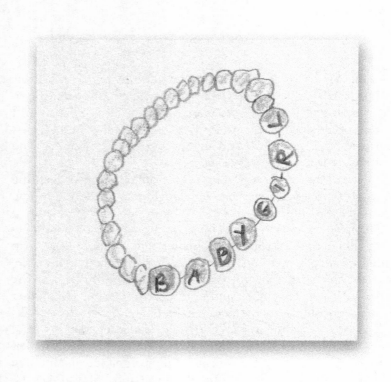

Episode 11

A Heart Starts Up Again

The woman was forty-five, with glowing skin, clear and unmarked. Tall, dark-haired, when she smiled it was easy to imagine her at twenty. Smiling now, she removed a snapshot of a young woman with dark hair from her purse and placed it facing me on the table. "My daughter," she said proudly.

It was the first picture she'd ever had of her daughter, and only the second time she'd seen her daughter's face since the moment, a quarter of a century earlier, when a door had been locked between them. Prior to labor, this woman had signed a placement agreement at the adoption agency where I used to work.

In earlier days, long before I worked there—she had been an agency client in 1966—the agency's doors had been kept open by the income earned from adoptions by childless couples who wanted babies like hers. A white infant (African-American families were not even served by this or most other agencies at that time), rather than an older child, she was what was actually referred to at one time as a "blue ribbon" baby. Her "alleged father" was described in the agency file, in terms more suitable for a kennel, as "Irish, Belfast descent, 6' tall, blue-eyed, medium build, long-boned, healthy, medium brown hair, green eyes, a college student, a talented painter and musician," and her mother, this woman, as "a college student, attractive and intelligent."

The services offered by the agency in the year I worked there included foster care and adoption services for older children, most of whom were African-American, and services to its former clients, the adult adoptees and birthmothers who wanted to find one another. I had been assigned the case of this woman and her daughter.

My social work education had unfortunately not included anything about adoption. I had, probably like most people, an unexamined belief that adoption was inherently a good thing, that it was about finding a safe and loving home for a child who desperately needed one.

Back in New Hampshire, prior to earning my MSW, I'd written a four-part newspaper series on child abuse and neglect; then, as a social work graduate student intern at a child welfare agency in Chicago, I'd provided counseling and home visits to families under court order for abuse and neglect. I'd also written a pamphlet for the National Committee for the Prevention of Child Abuse about child sexual abuse.

I'd stood in court in the Child Protection Division—a place certain to make anyone's heart ache—and listened to a judge order that a three-year-old boy have unsupervised weekend visits with the mother who had inflicted bruises on his face and body, and had refused to give him water when he was sick. He had deteriorated into a coma and nearly died, yet visits had been justified on the grounds of "family preservation."

It was nearly impossible to terminate the parental rights of that child's mother and father. The court was hopelessly overloaded. The state caseworker might or might not prepare papers properly. Witnesses might or might not show up. A public defender would be assigned to protect the parents' rights, a guardian-ad-litem to protect the child's. Hearings would be scheduled. And cancelled. And rescheduled. Years could pass while children across the country could live in foster care, like the "Cabbage Patch" dolls so popular at that time, until it was too late to be adopted. Or they would be returned home, perhaps to be further harmed, sometimes even killed. I was wary of inalienable parental rights.

But the story of this mother and her daughter, and the scores of stories I read about in agency files, and subsequently listened to from birthmothers and adult adoptees whom I later interviewed after I left the agency, were not about abuse and neglect. The babies available from the adoption agency in the past had not been in desperate need of a safe and loving home. Their mothers had not been abusive or neglectful—they were simply "unmarried."

After I'd seen how hard it was to terminate parental rights in court, I was shocked by the ease with which those rights had been ended in past years through adoption. No public defender, here, for the young women who were condemned by society for being "unmarried"; no guardian-ad-litem for the babies who were separated forever from their mothers.

Women like the one I was advising—who had been judged unfit only because of their marital status, and because of the "advice" of adoption caseworkers who were employed to find babies for childless couples—had, by merely signing their names, in a moment of great emotional stress and vulnerability, forever and irrevocably lost their children. And their children, like this woman's daughter, had lost their mothers.

In the basement storerooms of this century-old agency there was still an ancient card file with the names, hand-written in a spidery, old-fashioned style, of forgotten babies, long-since grown up and long-since dead, and there were numerous locked filing cabinets. These were off-limits to everyone except top staff. They held the files of famous people, I was told, or the adoptions by staff members, or by people who were on the board of directors. All the other files, thousands of them, were in warehouses, and at the time I worked there, were also overflowing several otherwise empty offices.

The only two long-time employees who held the mysteries of the storage and retrieval system in their heads were on medical leave. No one else was quite sure where all the files were, or how to get to them. Every day, at lunch, the kind-hearted woman who answered the phone requests from adoptees and their mothers told me of the ceaseless calls and her frustration at having to put them on waiting lists of over a year; sometimes she was unable even to tell adoptees if their adoption had taken place here.

But I had been easily able to find this case file that I had been assigned because it was stored on-site, having been opened many times over the past twenty-five years. The mother had repeatedly sent birthday cards, in case they could ever be delivered, and had even visited the agency to inquire about her daughter.

Opening the file was like falling down a rabbit hole into someone else's most private life and past. Here was the daughter's original birth certificate; on her amended birth certificate the mother's name had vanished and the adoptive parents' names been inserted. Here was the card sent by her adoptive family to the agency caseworker the first Christmas following the baby's adoption; also, a few baby photos; a doctor's report soon after birth ("healthy white female"); a verbatim account of the caseworker's few meetings and phone calls with the mother. Still fastened with tape to the manila folder was the baby's hospital baby bracelet.

I could read information forbidden to the people to whom it belonged, and what I read revealed both the lack of any meaningful help given to the mother, and the agency's transparent desire for her baby.

That baby, now twenty-five years old, had made persistent phone calls to the agency, which resulted in the assigning of her case to me, and eventually my finding her birthmother.

From our first phone conversation, the daughter was hungry to get every scrap of information she could about her mother. Each fact, no matter how ordinary, was a revelation to her. She told me that she felt she had no history. She had never even known her ethnicity.

She said she used to act as if she didn't care about having been adopted, insisting to others that she didn't have any interest in her natural family. But now that she was older, she felt that her vehemence had been necessary to cover up both her intense curiosity about her real parents and her anger at knowing nothing about them.

Once she admitted to herself that she was interested, she had so many questions. She had to have answers, even though her adoptive parents had said they were afraid of losing her if she found her mother, and her adoptive father was angry that it was even possible for her to search. He was of the opinion that all records should be burned.

She said she had always felt different from the rest of her adoptive family, and wondered if, when she found her birthmother and learned about her biological family, she would find a reason for this. She did not feel that her adoptive family had ever understood her, and she reported that while growing up she had had much conflict with her adoptive parents. She believed that her adoptive mother had not been well-suited to motherhood, but had adopted and raised two children because being a mother was the expected role of women. The young woman thought that her adoptive mother seemed much happier now that the children were grown and out of the house.

I had never considered how difficult, how painful, it would be to know nothing at all about where you came from. My daughter sometimes asked me to retell the story of her birth, settling happily near me to hear it all over again, and she could see, on our walls at home, the photographs of her grandmother, great-grandmother, and great-great-grandmother, all of whom she resembled.

But this young woman knew nothing at all. She resembled no one in her family. Her adoptive parents were infertile, as, indeed, they had been required to prove with a medical certificate in order to adopt her. She said—as I was also to hear from many other adoptees—that she sometimes felt she had come from another planet.

While I prepared what information I was permitted to give to her, I began trying to find her mother by following up the addresses she had so carefully sent to the agency over the years.

I hunted fruitlessly through telephone books for one address on the east coast, apparently the name of an organization. Later, the mother and I would realize that the organization's name had been entered incorrectly into her file. If that had been the only lead, neither I nor anyone else at the agency might ever have found her.

Luckily, the file indicated what college the mother had attended, and, luckily, that college had an updated alumni directory that included her, and, luckily, there was a friendly person at the alumni office willing to give me the address.

I sent the mother a note on the agency letterhead stating that I had important confidential information and asking her to call me. I was concerned that such an impersonal note would alarm her, but I was advised not to write more since I didn't know who might open the letter.

Several weeks went by with no response. She must have moved and left no forwarding address. Her daughter called me regularly to see if I was making any progress, and I was sorry each time to disappoint her. Finally, one Monday there was a pink telephone message slip in my agency mailbox. The mother had called over the weekend and left her number with the agency's answering service.

I dialed her number with trepidation. She answered at once, as though the phone was in her lap. I said, "The confidential information is that your daughter is looking for you." There was a big intake of breath at the other end of the receiver, then many minutes of sobbing.

When, finally, she could speak, she told me that as a nurse she'd had occasion to thump a person's chest to re-start a heart. "This is what your words have done for me," she said, "re-started my heart after twenty-five years."

I called the daughter. She cried with the same intensity as her mother. She told me later that when she drove to meet her mother and got a few feet from her mother's driveway she nearly chickened out. "I was afraid she'd cry and I wouldn't, that I'd just stand there with no feeling. But as soon as I saw her, I started crying. She had to help me out of the car. We're so alike!

We just looked and looked at each other. Her eyes seemed so familiar."

And the mother later told me, with serious eyes, and tenderness in her voice, "She let me hold her. It was quite a moment, to hold my baby for the very first time."

Episode 12

Transitions

On my daughter's thirteenth birthday, she'd made a card for me. She drew a tree with a heart as its fruit, and wrote, "Dearest Mother, Thank you for giving me life and letting me have this 13th spring."

⌣

I'm still getting used to my daughter being back from her father's, school starting, and regular life resuming. Yesterday I walked outside with her to see her off to middle school. She was wearing the peach-colored sweater her father gave her. Thirteen-and-a-half years old, a young woman ("all grown up" was the neighbor's polite way of putting it) on a street on an end-of-summer day, greeting her school friend. Long legs, fledgling feminine shape, all hope and eagerness. Our next-door neighbors are moving, and things are shifting. The familiarity of our old house is comforting—even its predictable mess.

I was glad I could be home when my daughter returned from school. She's still snuggling, in an awkward way—head first and less body contact. Her eyes are nearly level with mine,

91

and she has filled out. She was very blue over eighth-grade social life. "Everyone" likes a certain girl. Boys call to ask out "everyone" but her. Some of the girls are like sharp-toothed piranha, tearing flesh and drawing blood. She speaks with an intonation she never used before, because her previous spontaneous behavior has been replaced by the need to conform. Junior high is torture. A constant gnawing at her self-esteem. Lots of homework. Pimples. Her nose looks like it's been blistered. She chattered, and I listened, and made comforting sounds, and we had tea and cooked our favorite treat, tapioca pudding.

I'm visiting my son and his girlfriend's sweet first home together in Wisconsin—cozy cats and a cozy young man and woman. Table set for two, everything clean and orderly and stocked up. My son shows me his sock drawer, each pair rolled neatly.

What a difference from when my daughter and I visited him when he was sharing an apartment with two male roommates. We had recoiled from sleeping in his six-week-old sheets, but nevertheless we had to. And sleeping in the same bed with my daughter was like sleeping with a hamster out of its cage, and his three cats talked all night.

The bathtub was black with grime, and because only men lived there, the toilet seat, if down, was wet. My son thought I was being a prima donna to want clean sheets. ("No one's slept in them for four weeks and before that they were only used two weeks!")

But now, he and his girlfriend have cleaned their apartment nicely, and he's set up the bathroom light so that when you turn it on the radio plays. The two kittens have a basket with a blanket in it; mama cat has a favorite cushion. A neighbor across the way has hung a pot of pink and white impatiens in her window.

My son tells me sunset is his favorite time. A spot of floor is lit by the sun and mama cat likes to sit and blink in it. He's arranged a toy ball on a string hanging from a hook in the ceiling.

Just twenty-two, he and his gentle girlfriend are like their kittens in their basket. Except now that they've graduated from college, they face figuring out what to do in life, where to live, and, soon, likely separation from each other.

For me, parting has always been difficult and painful. I am like the mama cat who sits blinking in the spot of sun, not wanting it to fade. I'm here as a middle-aged mother, with another kitten, already half-grown, still with me.

It helps to see my grown child, to see what can happen after you let go. Sitting across from him at his pleasant table for two by the windows, I think, "Here he is, bobbing along high in the open sea, and the little harbor of home is practically out of sight." And I'm bobbing, too.

My daughter is moody and difficult lately. She says it's me. I think it's her.

It seems such a long time since I helped her dry her back after a shower, though she still sometimes asks me to tickle her back and tuck her into bed. She is more likely to tuck me in, as I nearly always am in bed before she is.

I see how little time we have left with her as belonging with us, so securely a part of our threesome. A mother's eyes can see into her daughter's past, but her daughter is looking at herself in the mirror dreaming of her future, trying to look through her present self to the young woman she is becoming.

She plopped onto our bed last night and wanted something from us. But it all went wrong, and her Valley Girl accenting of words made me cross, and her recital of the video she and her friend made (which I'd already told her I would watch, so especially didn't need to have her recite her description of it) also made me cross, so that I hurt her feelings, and this drove her out, which gave us privacy. But I didn't want it at the price of her feelings.

As she went out, she said, justifiably, "Whatever I say is wrong." Forty-six-year-olds are just in another realm of interests and conversations from nearly fourteen-year-olds.

93

How fast it all goes. I see ahead, sometimes, to no child at home, to her as a young woman, to my own old age. My mother got very sick when she was only fifty-three, and died when she was sixty-three. I don't know what being healthy and happy when you're old looks like. But I'm not my mother, and what happened to her—what she did to herself—isn't fated for me. I can make—I have made—different choices.

⌐

A few days ago we went to a Peruvian restaurant with friends and their two-and-a-half-year-old daughter, who was very charming. Sitting next to me was my once-upon-a-time-two-and-a-half-year-old, long-legged daughter, still putting her head on my shoulder, but nearly gone from childhood. I should prepare her with some pads to carry in her backpack, as she could start her period any day.

Yesterday I drove her and her friends to the movies, where she was to meet A Boy. Half her size, the boy belongs to a race of mini-men. They are far from the grown men who now glance at her on the street. Some don't stare. Others do. "I could consider this my first date," she said. And I, leaving her at the movies, was near tears. As it seems I often am these days. And last night, she said this mini-man had asked her to "go" with him, though what exactly that means she didn't know, nor did I. She was very pleased—thrilled, really, at reaching a sort of milestone.

⌐

Writing, on the back stoop at the cottage in Ellison Bay. I told my husband that after reading over my diaries I see I have the same themes over and over: "love you," "it's hard being a mother," "happy love," "upset with you," "Mother," "headache," "worries about children," "can't write," "can write," "work," "worries about money," "sweets," and "all other." "Which theme are you going to write about today?" he asked.

"Love you" and "headache gone," I replied.

94

We three watched a National Geographic special about a bizarre South American bird, the harpy eagle. Seeing all the astounding variety, intricacy, and adaptations of creatures, I think, could it all be mere chance? Yet also how cruel nature is—that sloth (world's creepiest creature) being killed by the eagle.

But is it so different from that predator on the highway, murdering a young woman who'd been driving alone and because of car trouble had to pull over? Except the eagle fed the sloth to its young, and that murderer killed for perverse pleasure. Predators can pluck you right off a tree where you're sitting blinking your eyes in the sun.

And for myself, even in Ellison Bay, I've turned back, while out for an afternoon walk down the road, because of the appearance of a man I've seen before, walking—that man with a ghostly face.

It is a miracle I have been able to stop smoking. I have a stray impulse this morning and it makes me realize what torture it always was to resist the urge. It is as if you are being tugged by some invisible force. What a blessing, how amazing, to not have that tugging at me day and night, to have, even, almost forgotten what it was like. And to sit in clean air with a calm heart and clear lungs, drinking coffee.

Last night after dinner I took a shower before we were going out for cherry pie. My husband had gone for a walk in the dark and returned saying he'd been to the end of the dock and it was sublime. So the two of us returned there. Down Cedar Road, it was pitch-black as soon as we walked past the one street light. I was frightened and nearly thrown off-balance by how dark it was. Then, on through a path opening through the trees I saw the stars—like a meadow of wildflowers.

All the tourists who'd been staying in the three or four rental houses there are gone, so there were no lights on, and there was no moon. Only a single boat tied at the dock and a family's voices coming over the water. We went to the end of the dock and my husband pointed out Cassiopeia.

⌣

Back home. This morning there's a winter storm warning— "near-blizzard" conditions—and dangerous cold. I will be glad to pick my daughter up from school and I'm feeling happy to be able to be an "at-home" mother today. Yesterday when she brought a friend home with her, I made muffins and tea. Late in the day, at near-dark, I went to the dry cleaners and the public library. I've seldom been at those places at that time of day because of work, but now that I don't have to go to a daily job, I am so glad I can write at home and work part-time in my therapy office. I came back from the library with a little stack of books. My husband gave me a beautiful leather weight to hold a book open. He had my initials stamped on it.

⌣

My husband's father left us some money and so we could take two trips. On Christmas Eve, on a television in a little one-story motel called "The Silver Saddle" in Sante Fe, New Mexico, my husband and I are watching the Pope say Mass. We drove through the Sangre de Cristo Mountains, and ate dinner in a restaurant that had a crackling fire place. For the first time ever, we are having this holiday away from my son and daughter, who are at their father's. The Pope, nobody's father, kisses some children.

We went to the little adobe sanctuary at Chimayo, a kind of healing shrine. It has several small rooms off the main one, and a basin of holy dirt. The walls are hung with icons, rosaries and "Milagros"—the little tin amulets representing the part of the body that needs healing: a leg, a knee, a heart—and photographs of children (who were healed? who died?); a faded and nearly-unreadable photocopy of a photograph of a wild-looking man who disappeared several months ago; hand-lettered praises and poems; full-size crutches. Offerings, in gratitude for a healing.

I bought two Milagros to take home: a tin head (depression, headaches, fatigue) for me; and a tin heart (arrhythmia) for my husband. I lit candles. A big one for my client who has two young children and adenocarcinoma of the lung; one for my three-year-old child client; one for the children awaiting adoption; and another for the child nobody wanted. An extra candle for whoever might need a guardian angel.

Then we spent one night visiting friends in North Carolina. Their two-year-old boy, just up from his nap, came into the room where we were still in bed on a convertible couch. He was so close to me, I could smell his baby-scent and feel the heat from

his head. His eyes were just at my eye-level, and his energy field was so intense and his life force so strong it was practically visible, like a light ray. His presence was like a sort of visitation.

Then we came to stay a few days in this beautiful old resort in North Carolina, and now, just at this moment, in comes a room-service breakfast with a flower, newspaper, tablecloth, and the waiter is pouring my coffee! It's so delicious to be pampered! I'm kind of ashamed of my pleasure in it. But I think of the dying words of someone's friend, told to us, "I only regret my economies."

It would be great for us to travel as much as we can, in our future. It's lovely to have a friend like my husband who thinks, as I do, that it is fun to read and write in a public library, who shares the idea that happiness is traveling with a little zipped bag containing paper clips, eraser, tiny stapler, and miniature scissors. He said last night, "I'm too happy. I don't like to be so happy."

We ate lunch with friends, had a long walk and cool drink on the terrace afterward. Now, back in our hotel room, my husband naps. I'm sitting at the window, watching the light changing outside, and the world itself changing. The sunlight has receded, and tomorrow is our last day. Everything passes—the daylight, a vacation, life. Darkness is coming and I haven't lit even the smallest electric lamp against it yet. I'm kept here at the window by my wish to hold back time.

on naps ...
from the team setups and in
thoughts —my wrist to hold
back time

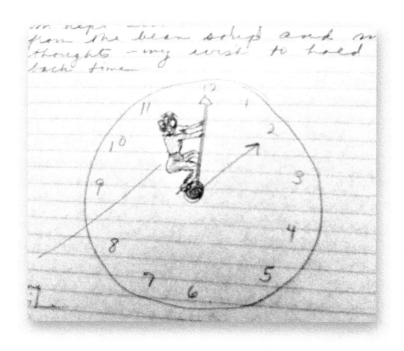

DISEASES OF WOMEN:

A MANUAL OF

GYNECOLOGY

DESIGNED ESPECIALLY FOR THE USE OF

STUDENTS AND GENERAL PRACTITIONERS.

BY

F. H. DAVENPORT, A.B., M.D.,

ASSISTANT PROFESSOR IN GYNECOLOGY, HARVARD MEDICAL SCHOOL; ASSIST-
ANT SURGEON TO THE FREE HOSPITAL FOR WOMEN, BOSTON.

THIRD EDITION, REVISED AND ENLARGED.

WITH 156 ILLUSTRATIONS.

LEA BROTHERS & CO.,
PHILADELPHIA AND NEW YORK.
1898.

Episode 13

Upsets and Comforts

I'm taking my ugly mood out for breakfast, hiding in the farthest back booth of a diner with a book and someone waiting on me. You'd have to throw chunks of meat through bars to me today— I have PMS, manifested by two ugly pimples (evidencing my true nature) and a savage mood which erupted at my daughter last night and made me slam a door. I'd had it. I was angry at both her and my husband and wanted to leave and go to a hotel (maybe this is why, in some places, menstruating women were kept in separate quarters).

A few days ago, my friend listened to me reading some of what I have been writing, and she made clucking sounds of understanding. I realized I'd read this piece only to my husband. She said, "Men don't know anything about it." I've carried her response around with me all day like a little hearth at which I can warm myself.

Sunny, so sunny it hurts your eyes, as the ground is completely white from yesterday's late blizzard. It was a white-out with a sideways wind yesterday, so everything was cancelled. Six girls are sleeping on cushions in the living room like inhabitants of Pompeii, struck not dead, but (mercifully) quiet—by the hand of sleep.

A window shade hangs halfway down. A chair is pushed against a door. I last heard them about 2 a.m. What a cultural phenomenon, this "slumber party." What a culture, these fourteen-year-old girls. Like sharks in a feeding frenzy, yet also maternal and sisterly. One foments strife and spreads vitriol; another bakes a birthday cake for my daughter.

⌐

In downtown Chicago it was misty. I felt wrapped up in the city's coat. After looking up genealogy information, I smiled, coming down the Newberry Library's interior marble steps from the reading room with its lit green lamps on its long, polished wood tables, pleased because of the beauty and order of libraries, the polished brass door handles with "N" in script, the tall Japanese-style dried flower arrangements, the mist outside the windows, closing us in even further in the protected comfort of civilization, books, quiet, and peace.

Outside, pleasure at being free and alone to stroll those nearby blocks and dream of living there. I pass a house exactly suited to my dreams—a dollhouse Victorian that causes me to squeal out loud. Nearby, a coffee shop, a bookstore, people walking little dogs on leashes, a dead-end street paved with red bricks. The tops of the skyscrapers, only a few blocks away, disappear in the high mist, and the street and shop lights shine. Waiting to cross a street I smell the perfume of a woman next to me; there's something familiar about it—Mother? And I think, "I'm perfectly happy."

Later, back home, while driving my daughter and her friend somewhere, these young, kind of thuggish girls saying "like go" and "like said" and swooning from their need to listen to a very particular radio station (which I decided served the purpose of a sort of outer space signaling device sending signals to all teenage receiver brains), I longed for the library's peaceful, quiet rooms.

⌣

It's three years since I quit smoking. Ten cigarettes a day times three hundred and sixty-five days a year equals three thousand six hundred and fifty cigarettes times three years equals ten thousand nine hundred fifty cigarettes that I have not smoked. If it was twenty cigarettes a day, one pack, it would be twenty-one thousand nine hundred cigarettes. What a horrifying thought! So no matter the weight I gain, I am grateful.

⌣

My fourteen-year-old daughter is notably relaxed and happy, chattering, "I'm happy it happened because it wasn't the end of our relationship; it brought you and me closer, don't you think?" We both cried last night, bumped out of our seats by the turbulence of adolescence and the big changes besetting us, but we did end up closer. A half-box of wadded-up Kleenex full of our tears is now in the kitchen trash can.

Our old life is over, our long old years of babyhood and childhood and the toys, the drawings, her hair ornaments, doll house. It's not a dollhouse now but a girlfriend's unchaperoned full-size house she moved herself around in—a world about which she lied to me, and that girl was said to be having sex with boys who sneaked in a basement window.

Tonight, because my daughter is grounded, she and I listen to jazz upstairs. I think of all the nights we used to listen, the three of us, when she was eleven, even twelve, but that's over. Much is over and changed. And now my son, too, will be leaving his college town in Wisconsin, and that will be another bump.

"What do I want?" asks the therapist I talked with. How about turning back the clock and un-doing all my mistakes; pulling out every thorn my unawareness and bad choices drove into the tender flesh of others, especially my children? I want, so, to be a good mother, and we only have four years left with my daughter at home.

I had a dream of three graves planted with flowering clocks, each set at different times—and see they are my mother's, mine, and my daughter's.

Always, when my period comes, relief; and comfort in its regularity, like the sunrise or other immutable natural event, though, at forty-six, no longer immutable. I know its arrival means relief from tension, an explanation for recent upsets, and a truce. My daughter and I are menstruating together. My period is late, hers is early. The family works, then, like the interlocking gears of a clock.

My son is gone to California and next week to China. I feel less anxious than I used to for his safety, feel less the tearing feeling of parting, the wish to keep him—because he's a man, though a young one, and because I realize I have to let go. I've had him for twenty-three years and hope to have him many more, in a new way; hope to see him grow to be my age. I wrote him once, on a birthday card, "You came into my life to teach me about love." But he's not my baby, or my child, but a man who needs to grow up more and who is part of a large world. So off he goes, to China. And I'm grateful I'm not sending him off, in uniform, to war, as so many mothers have had to do.

⌣

I'm blue on a Friday night. My husband is in Laguna Beach and I wish I were with him in the lovely-sounding California town instead of stuck here with three teenage girls who view me as an instrument to serve them. And who are plotting about going to someone's apartment with no father there but six girls and two boys.

I'm tired of worrying about "Where?" and "With whom?" and "How?" and "Please turn down the music!" and "Would you please do the dishes without my having to ask you again?" and "I'm sorry for looking at you the wrong way" and "Wait! I just cashed a check and have no money—why do I suddenly have only $13? Oh, the shampoo and the eye-makeup remover and the acne medication, right, then the money for the overdue library book and the shoes, and yes, I know you need a bathing suit."

All the solitary pleasures of having finished my book manuscript about adoption and sent it off to an agent, and of my work with others in my own therapy office, dim, sputter, and go out. I'm alone on a dark Friday night, this time unhappy not because I'm home with a small child or waiting for a man but because my daughter is a teenager and . . .

My husband does not understand my perspective—what it's like to be left at home "holding down reality" while your other is being celebrated. I'm here for him and my daughter so they can be not here. He wishes I "had more resources." They both wish I "had more resources" as long as I continue to be their primary "resource."

My husband is going to flip out when I tell him the cost of the efficient and expensive vacuum cleaner I want to buy. It does seem a stupid way to spend money, but I want, for once, to buy the best. I still have my grandmother's Hoover vacuum cleaner.

He said, of my daughter buying perfume, how pointless when she has so much and I replied someone might say of him why buy all those books when you haven't read the ones you've got? And he said books are good for my soul and I said so perfume is good for her soul. "You think?" he replied doubtfully.

What sort of soul is mine, to be gladdened by a green, German-designed vacuum cleaner?

⌢

We arrived in Ellison Bay last night, our first trip of the year up here. I could hardly wait to get up for coffee in the old white ironstone mug. I cut a nearly-closed, deep-coral tulip to put in the turquoise glass vase; closer to me, to smell, are two hyacinths and a daffodil.

Apple blossom from our tree 5/03

The day didn't hold a moment that wasn't happy. Arriving on the peninsula, we stopped at the restaurant with the gazebo, where we had cabbage soup, frosty pink lemonade with a sharp yellow lemon on the rim of the glass, and read the newspaper we'd brought with us. Then, as we drove down Cedar Road, there, suddenly appearing before us, was our red cottage, dwarfed by the tall trees; waiting for us, after the long winter and cold early spring.

We open the door to our two small downstairs rooms, reminding me of that miniature world fashioned inside a hinged walnut shell I'd once seen as a child. The cottage preserves the past, like a time capsule. Here is the wood washstand that once stood in my house in New Hampshire; here, the teapot and one cup and saucer I'd kept from that wedding china.

Here is a wicker chair from my parents' house, and some framed botanical prints of my grandmother's. Here, that turquoise cracked robin's egg my daughter once found, and a small rock she'd painted with a face. And the ceramic lamp shaped like a pony that I'd found at a nearby second-hand store, and the old school desk.

In the tiny room with the water-heater, my writing room, there is the old wooden desk and chair that, during my depression, I'd sponge-painted green and pink; and a bookcase I'd painted yellow, with flowers.

In the little back entry hall there is ancient flowered linoleum, and the stairs we painted a soft blue-gray, with silver stars on the walls, as I sang "Let's make a stairway to the stars," and a framed piece of sheet music ("Wishing Moon"), and at the top of the stairs, our bedroom: a pottery lamp with red cherries and a pink shade, and an old wooden dresser on the drawers of which I'd painted a robin with its rusty-colored breast, a robin's egg, and a yellow-and-gray tufted bird. On the top, an old shaving mirror, a box containing feathers that my husband's sister had found once when visiting.

And beyond our bedroom, my daughter's. A blue-and-gray braided round rug, a small white metal bed with a pink chenille spread, the moon and stars on a deep blue sky that she'd painted on her wall when she was younger. A toy cradle, with a doll in it.

From a Letter to My Mother

PART THREE

Things are different for women now, Mother. It had only just begun when you died. Your granddaughter is in law school. She doesn't even know how to iron! I remember learning from you, wanting to learn, how to iron the shoulders of a blouse (those white blouses we wore).

She lives with a man without being married, and no one thinks a thing about it. She has so much freedom. If she was single, and if she wanted to, she could have a sperm bank send a vial to her doctor, and become a mother without even meeting a man. I'm not so sure this is a good idea, but I'm not sure it's so different from my first, very brief marriage, out of which came my son.

It's nothing unusual now for a woman to be a lawyer, a doctor, a professional something. To live a whole life without being a mother. Or, if a mother, to have help. Those who can afford it can have a nanny; those, like I was, who can't, at least have daycare, even though daycare was brand-new when my son was a toddler, at the time that you died.

Not that it's easy to have a professional life, to work and be a mother, but it's possible. It's that a woman is not expected, anymore, only to be someone's wife, someone's mother. She can be what she chooses to be. If, of course, she has the resources. If she can obtain the education, and isn't slain by poverty or violence, or misled by her own loneliness, her own emptiness, to have a child to keep her company, to fill her up. If she doesn't trap herself.

But at least it's not societal standards that are trapping her. There is birth control available, and—as of this writing, anyway—abortion, if she really messes up. She has choices.

But you, Mother—you had some, too. Birth control was available in your day. You managed not to get pregnant, in fact, for a number of years. Then, in 1935, you did. And in 1938. In 1941, in 1944, and in 1946. I understand from my sister that there were also three other pregnancies that ended in miscarriage, one that you maybe even aborted, under the guise of a miscarriage.

Five children. Eight pregnancies. And you hadn't even converted from Episcopalian to Catholic, yet. What were you thinking, Mother? My father couldn't support one child, much less five. If your mother's rich second husband hadn't given my father a job, what would you have done? I talked to her stepson, who had been my father's boss for many years, and he told me that my father never would have kept that job if it weren't for your mother. He told me that my father wanted to be a college professor, but wasn't willing to put in the work to become one, so he just acted as if he was one.

You really trapped yourself, marrying him and having us. My oldest brother's first wife, your daughter-in-law, told me that you "held everything together with bubble gum." She thought that you were determined to stay with my father to prove that your mother was wrong about him.

I did ask you once why you had so many children. "Because I hated being an only child, and I didn't want any of you to be an only child," you replied. Well, Mother, it would only have taken two, then. Not five. Not eight. It wasn't as if you especially liked children! You didn't understand children, had no earlier experience with them, were not suited. You should have been a college professor or a writer, you should have had the life your middle daughter, my sister, had. Her lovely study with a fireplace, Mother, tall windows overlooking green trees, shelves of books, a Persian rug. There's music, peace, spaciousness for thought. I often wish that you had had such a room.

You could have. You were such a good student, you were an honors college graduate, you were enrolled in graduate school in English. You gave it all up and married my father. I am so sorry.

Well, maybe the last three of us children were accidents. Although I don't understand how such an intelligent woman could have three accidental pregnancies. I know that I was an accident, because you told me. That wasn't very thoughtful,

Mother. Even though you added "but you were loved." Many years after you died, as I was writing my book about you, I found that letter you wrote to your mother when you were pregnant with me, calling me "an Act of God" and saying that you were "perfectly settled" in your own mind, that "there wasn't anything to be done about it." And I, two months away from my birth, was in your womb, asleep, or moving about in my amniotic world, while you were writing that letter.

By then, your oldest son was eleven, and my father was beating him. You were in what you wrote to your mother was "a good old rat-race" with your oldest daughter. You said, in that paper about religion that you wrote many years later, that "things got awfully daily and on the whole pretty meaningless. I had a fine husband and five nice children, but what were we all doing here, and why, and to what purpose?" Wifehood and motherhood, Mother, had not filled—could not fill—that emptiness you must have felt inside.

So you turned to religion. I guess you thought it was the only solution. You used the Church's teachings to keep on beating your own feelings down, to keep denying them, converting them into their opposite, swallowing them. Oh, I don't want to think about it all, about religion and how it put you down. About that priest, and washing and ironing his priestly garments. It makes me sick.

Choices, choices. I keep getting stuck on people's choices. I used to feel more sympathy for some others than I do now. More understanding of their confusion, of the underwater currents that drive them (us) to choose badly—disastrously!—for themselves (ourselves). But the older I get, the more often I say to myself, "What did they (we?) expect?" The homeowner who builds too close to the riverbank and gets flooded. The man who cheats on his wife, leaves her to do all the parenting, and then wonders why she thinks ill of him. I guess it's easier to feel sympathy when a person's bad choices only involved suffering for him or her, and not for children. Or when you see that someone has been so handicapped by poverty, abuse, and lack of opportunities that she or he cannot be held responsible.

113

Because there wasn't a choice. There was only the stark, daily, need to survive. That's one thing.

But isn't it another when someone is—like you were, Mother—educated? Privileged? When your whole life lay before you, and you chose my father? Chose eight pregnancies, and cigarettes, and alcohol, and tranquillizers? Chose a version of God that told you that you were "not worthy to gather up the crumbs under 'His' (always that capital 'H') table?"

I guess it just piled up, Mother, huh? First you married my father, even though—maybe partly because—your mother so disapproved. She was mean, and yet she was right about him, Mother! That must have been galling. Did you ever let yourself admit she was right?

I don't think so. You couldn't. If you had admitted that, then the whole house of cards, your whole life—the five children, all those years of marriage—would have come tumbling down. And it wasn't as if you could have gotten divorced, really. My father was a poor provider, married. How could you have managed, divorced? Well, women did. Women always have. But—you loved him. You didn't want to be divorced. But Mother—how could you let him mistreat your children?

But I'm lecturing you, squawking at you like a jay, as my husband once wrote of me, in a poem. And lecturing is something you never did to me. I appreciate that, Mother. That you weren't on my back, the way some mothers are. But I'm afraid it might be because I was the last child, and you were tired, and depressed, and I'd just have to take care of myself.

I did. I was an awfully good child, wasn't I? It makes me sad for myself, now, to think how I must have tried to be good so that you'd love me, so that it would be easier for you. A child ought to be the apple of her mother's eye, just for being born, just for being. I never felt that—though I didn't know I didn't, for decades and decades, because you can't miss what you've never experienced, as my friend who had been a nun said about sex.

I'm sad I never experienced that feeling of being the apple of your eye. You must have experienced it, because you surely were the apple of your father's eye. But then you lost him. He left on that night train, heading, with your mother, for a brief trip, and came back in a coffin. And once you weren't her little baby, your mother was the most difficult kind of mother one could have. Maybe the kind of mother who would never forgive you for the pain of her labor.

Your mother saw you, always, only as a reflection of herself. I see in the old photographs how she over-dressed you, her little doll. I remember you telling me how distressing it was to you that she insisted that you wear white stockings when all the other little girls were wearing black. Too bad for her that her little doll grew up, got ideas of her own, married my father, and became a "Dem." She'd make you pay, forever, your mother would, and did, by lecturing and squawking—a whole flock of jays in one person. She'd tell you how to wear your hair, what to say, how to act, and everything you did wrong, which was everything you didn't do as she would have done. You were her ever-lasting personal project. Talk about lecturing.

Well, Mother, maybe it was the emotional bruises from a mother like that that made you hands-off with me, and not just neglect. I'd like to think so. I appreciated not being criticized by you. So I guess I should stop criticizing you and try to understand you.

Episode 14

In the Beauty Parlor

Back in Chicago, I'm the only customer left in the beauty parlor, where I am having a rare manicure after getting my hair cut. It's the end of the day, and the four women employees are relaxing. One is giving herself a manicure, one is giving me one, one is looking through a magazine of hair styles, and one is at the computer.

The woman looking at the magazine holds a page out to the others and says, "Here's the color I want to do my hair."

The co-worker who is giving herself a manicure looks, says, "What, you're getting highlights?"

"No," the first woman replies, "Chunks. I want chunks of number three."

"You don't want chunks! Why do you want chunks?" says her co-worker. "Get highlights. Chunks make you look like a skunk! And number three is too light. Didn't you just do a number five?"

"Nah, I'm number seven," says the first woman. She goes to get the numbered hanging cards with swatches of synthetic hair of different colors. She points to them in turn. "See this? I used to be a five. Now I'm a seven. I'm gonna get chunks of number three."

Her co-worker shrugs. Her nails are now under a little nail-drying fan. She examines them, turning her head right, then left, the way women look at a baby's face. "I like this! It's kind of purple," she says.

Sitting at the next manicure table, she turns to glance at me. My nails are being examined with intense scrutiny by a young woman in her late twenties with very short hair slicked straight back behind her ears. Her entire ears, in fact, all of the cartilage above the lobe, are studded with small earrings, like an upholstered chair.

I admire the other woman's nails, and ask, "What color is that?"

"Berry Buffalo Bingo," she answers, turning her face toward me with ready friendliness. I see that one of her eyes seems to be artificial; its movement does not quite synchronize with the other. She has been injured, somehow, in her past.

"Nice!" I say. I've gathered from listening to their conversation that she is about to go on a trip somewhere. "Where are you going?" I ask.

"On a Carnival cruise," she replies. "With my girlfriend and her cousin."

"Oh," I say. "That sounds really nice. I hear there's tons of good food on a cruise."

She looks anxious. "Yeah, I'm gonna have to be careful about what I eat—I don't want to gain weight," she says.

"The heck with weight, enjoy yourself," I say.

She relaxes. "Yeah, that's right."

"Where do you go on the cruise?" I ask. My manicurist is bent over my hand, removing tiny pieces of uneven cuticle.

"I'm not sure of the names of the places," she answers, looking anxious again. "Those saint places, those islands."

"Someplace nice and warm," I say.

"Yeah," she replies.

"Are you packed?" asks the woman who's been looking at a magazine.

"Unh uh, I'm gonna do that tonight," she says.

"That won't take more than ten minutes," says the manicurist. "Throw the stuff in a bag."

There's a companionable silence among us. Then my manicurist speaks, "I'm gonna do my hair a number one."

The women make noises of interest and enthusiasm.

"You'd look great as a platinum!" says the magazine reader.

My manicurist comes alive. "I was, once, you know, and it looked good. But you have to color it every two weeks or roots show, and I got sick of it."

"It turns green," says the magazine reader.

"Yeah, it was a pain," sighs the manicurist, who is painting my nails with short, sure strokes.

The woman who has been looking at the computer suddenly announces, "70 percent of my clients are Virgos!"

I look up and say, "No kidding? How do you know that?"

"I keep files on all my customers," she answers.

My manicurist nods. "Like gets like." She adds, "You always get a certain sign. Like my father's a Sagittarius, my son's one, my ex, he's a Sag too." She shakes her head.

The woman at the computer sighs and says, "Yeah, well, men. They're all born under the Sign of the Jerk."

Episode 15

The Light in Italy

"Starry, starry night!" I sang at the open window, looking over the lights of the Italian hill town spread out below me, and above at the dark bucket of sky spilling stars. Earlier, we had eaten fresh bread, prosciutto sliced as thin as skin, and fat, oily, nearly sweet black olives for dinner: me, my husband, my fifteen-year-old daughter, each at our own pace, as we made ourselves at home for a two-week stay in our rented furnished apartment.

I arranged the fruits in one blue bowl, the vegetables in another, admiring again the dusky green fresh figs, the perfectly oval onion, the deep red tomatoes with their green stems. Then, singing "O Sole Mio!" I washed some of my clothes in the sink, and found a drying rack in the kitchen—not able, yet, to figure out how the Italians hang their clothes to dry across the window, in the sun and breeze. Later, I saw it was a simple pulley, but in the overwhelming rush of perceptions at being in a foreign country—my first time in Italy—it seemed to me as if the clothes hung by magic.

I bathed in the white porcelain tub, with a view of warm red tiled roofs, and the terrace of a large house (a "palazzo," my husband said) above us with vivid, deep-pink blossoms in earthen pots. He smiled at me as I came out damp and fragrant from the bath, wrapped in a white towel. Later, to please my daughter, we strolled once again before settling in for the night, an entirely new stroll from the one we had taken when we had first arrived this afternoon, down different narrow medieval cobblestoned streets.

The stone pavings echoed with the sounds of voices—adult and child—speaking Italian, with Italian television, and with the whining of the motor scooters. The narrow lanes were redolent with the scents of dinners and with the odor of the hot stone walls of the houses and paving. A man on a motor scooter with his small son seated within the circle of his arms passed us and went round a corner, then, as we, too, rounded the corner, we saw the same small boy, his helmet on, being swung by the arms by his older brother. Closer still, we saw his mother, laughing; and a small dog with a wagging tail—even the dogs were friendly in Italy.

We passed an old man sitting in a wooden kitchen chair, his hands on the handle of his cane; behind him was a rose bush against a low stone wall, over which there was another vista of the steep streets of this hill town and its cascade of red tiled roofs and flowerpots. I nodded and smiled broadly to the old man, feeling faintly apologetic for being American, for walking down his street.

We passed by the child-sized door of a stone house, its handle a brass hand, polished to a deep luster and smoothness by countless years of hands upon it, and above the brass hand, a brass letter-slot, also small enough to be a child's. Everywhere, potted deep-pink or red geraniums, and the houses pale-yellow, mustard, pink, or peach.

This small Italian town was pleasing to look at, not only because it was so old and worn smooth, like a child's beloved toy, but because of its proportions; it was meant to accommodate people rather than cars. Only a few of the streets were wide enough for even one small car. It felt like we had been set down on the stage set of a medieval play, and that as we walked we were actors on the play's five sets: the market square ("piazza," my husband said), with its stone clock tower and fountain of clear, cold water gushing from the mouth of a sculpted lion's head; the cathedral and its dusty, hot square; the other piazza of the tourist office and post office; the convent within whose thick walls was a placid courtyard with potted bright flowers; and, rising above it all, at the top of the steep hill upon which the town was built, the fortress, or the "rocca." The entire town could be traversed by foot in less than an hour.

On our own street was a cobbler's shop, really only one small room right off the street, where the cobbler worked in his overalls, bent over and hammering, just like Geppetto in the children's story "Pinocchio"; a food shop with its salami rolls and olives; another one-room shop whose narrow front windows displayed demure, large, women's underpants and garters.

My daughter, whose attention had been thoroughly captured the minute we arrived in Rome three days earlier, said that compared to Italy "at home everyone and everything is ugly and mean." She was responding to the beauty, the scale of life in this small town, and the sense of community that did not exist at home. Here there seemed always to be people of all ages walking on the stone streets, greeting one another, sitting in the cafes and gelato shops, in a slow, beautiful ballet. It seemed so welcoming, so reassuring, in a way, to live for a few weeks in such a community.

The flight from home had been non-stop, disconcerting. If it was possible to get on a plane at home and, without even stopping, get off in Rome, a place real to me only from long-ago schoolbooks, it almost seemed possible to get on at home and get off in the past, or in the future.

There hadn't been three open seats together, so my daughter and I took the two that were adjacent, and my husband was in a seat several rows behind. I had been both glad and sorry to be next to her because, when near me, she talks nearly all the time, and, after decades of being a mother to my daughter and my son, while I was glad that she wanted to talk to me, I treasured the occasions when I could think uninterrupted; I savored the luxury of silence.

I appreciated—even envied—my daughter's ability to laugh at almost everything. Hadn't I read somewhere that children laugh three hundred times a day? Especially because my husband, an essentially serious person, laughed infrequently. Laughing with my daughter was a great pleasure and a strong bond between us. But there were times when the laughing became irritating, because nothing escapes her sharp eye, especially nothing about me, her mother.

She and I had meekly accepted all the offerings of the flight—doll-sized meals, consisting of, I said to her, "Food-like substances," some of which, she'd retorted, looked like "chopped baby limbs"; hot cloths to clean our hands; headphones, pillows and blankets. She had immediately spilled her can of orange juice between her legs, soaking her denim shorts. Spilling things—which we both do frequently—is a reason for laughing. I was glad, then, that I, not my husband, was sitting next to her. He gets disapproving when we spill and reminds us to put napkins on our laps or lean over our plates instead of flinging food about ourselves as we talk excitedly. And when he gets disapproving, I feel myself withdraw.

She hadn't spilled juice on anyone but herself, after all. And she was being a good sport about it, considering she was going to be spending nine hours in sticky wet shorts because she hadn't packed (as I had told her to) extra shorts in her carry-on bag. It was good that she chattered so much, and that we'd laughed. I hadn't wanted to think about the fact that we were hurtling through dark space, thousands and thousands of feet above the known, beloved world.

Eventually, she'd fallen asleep, her face against a small pillow on my shoulder, her long legs tucked up against me. I wished that I, too, could sleep, like my fellow passengers, some with their mouths hanging open. For me, sleep had come only in fragments and chaotic dreams incorporating the "ding, ding" of the flight attendants' call buttons. I had felt too exposed to sleep, like some small animal on a bare rock; I couldn't find a safe corner in which to curl up, and my elbows ached from holding them away from the person in the seat on my other side, a woman whose flesh overflowed into my already too-small space, and who, earlier, had wanted to pass the time by talking, a fate I had escaped by taking out my Italian phrasebook and pretending to study it.

I'd been trying to learn enough Italian to at least be able to ask simple questions ("Where is the bathroom?") and to order food. I would have liked to be able to get myself about without my husband's help. He had traveled in Europe before, and knew Italian, but I had only been "overseas" once, with a group, when I was nineteen. I'd borrowed language tapes from the library, but kept getting distracted by the English accents of the speakers, and my daughter would fall over laughing when she'd walk into the room where I was saying out loud, "Could I have some hot watah please?" in the English accent of the tape's instructor, instead of repeating the Italian phrase. We had amused ourselves repeating imaginary English phrases to each other like, "Pahdon me while I vomit on your shoes!"

Because my hearing was not good, I often mixed up similar-sounding words, which didn't help when trying to learn a language. My daughter and I had begun collecting certain nonsensical phrases I thought I had heard in the course of a day, such as, "Could I have a bowl of udders?" and "A melon is a very pleasant thing to ride on." She laughed and laughed at me. I usually didn't mind it, but sometimes I got tired of being found ridiculous. Growing up as the youngest of five children, I had sometimes been cruelly teased by my siblings. When I'd tried to stand up for myself, I'd been taunted with being "easily offended."

My husband, the oldest of three children, was used to being the leader. He was always leading and I am always following. Though grateful for his skill at finding his way around a new place, I also often felt, in contrast, inept. I was capable of leading but, with him, I seldom had the chance. He knew so much about what I thought of as "the world"—languages, history, how to fix things, how to tie knots. What was it I knew?

When my daughter was eleven she wrote a description of me: "My mom is a social worker and she works at a hospital. She likes to read and loves children, puppies, and kittens. She's afraid of bats and large birds, and she hates mice. She loves my brother, my stepfather, and myself. My mom has a great sense of humor, and my friends sometimes envy me. She's a lot of fun, she's like my best friend. One time when my stepdad was out of town my mom and I had a pig dinner. A pig dinner is when you eat without using any utensils. That was a lot of fun. I love my mom, and I hope to be like her someday." I'd saved that precious note, knowing she would not always feel that way about me as she got older.

My husband had thrown over, for me, his own careful and orderly life, in what was, I only realized much later, a most uncharacteristic manner. But choosing me had also meant choosing my daughter, two-and-a-half at the time, and my son, eleven. I sometimes wondered, when my husband seemed tired of our heedlessness, when he reminded us about our napkins, if he missed his childless former life. Though my son had grown and gone, life with a fifteen-year-old was noisy. The phone rang continually; friends tramped in and out of the house. My daughter, like a dandelion, dropped evidence of herself everywhere — shoes flung off, an empty pop can, piles of wet towels, barrettes, books and papers.

And the very traits that had attracted my husband and me to each other could now at times irritate us. He had sought passionate feeling; I, too — and steadiness. But perhaps I, and my daughter, provided too much turbulence. Her temperament and mine were similar, and what began as a conversation between mother and daughter might quickly spiral into an argument. My husband circled us when this happened, his arms crossed tensely before his chest. After we flew apart, he'd talk quietly to one, then the other. It was his calm, his ballast, that permitted us to rock the boat of our re-constituted family so forcefully. We depended on his controlled emotion, yet also regarded it, and his need for order, as foreign, as if we were the natives of a country he was only visiting.

In Rome, we'd settled into our hotel room, then gone out to walk around for several hours; my husband first, my daughter following him, then me, single file, because the streets were too narrow to walk together. My daughter at fifteen was like a fledgling bird, nearly big enough to fly but still content to gaggle by her parents, still wanting to open her mouth and be fed. The Roman men, however, saw her as a woman. Their heads turned as if on swivels when she passed by, and as soon as we were on a piazza my husband and I walked protectively on either side of her. I was reminded of the TV nature shows she and I liked to watch, of one in which lions stalked, waiting for the vulnerable calf to leave, for a moment, its mother's side, then the snap of jaws, the dragging away of the catch.

She stayed close. When a man sat himself on a marble seat at the edge of the fountain opposite our table on the Piazza Navona, opened his legs, and just stared at her, she'd turned to me to laugh in amazement. Conspiratorial in our femaleness, under the protection of husband and stepfather, we elbowed each other and giggled at the men preening and strutting like exotic birds around us.

After another day of sightseeing in Rome, we'd taken the train to the hill town where my husband was teaching at a conference. I was discouraged by my attempts to speak Italian. I'd asked for a sandwich made of "man" (uomo) instead of "egg" (uovo). And I could not figure out the money. So that night, in our rented apartment, after we'd returned from our stroll, while my daughter listened to music on her headphones, I'd lain backwards on the bed, my bare feet flat against the cool wall, and looked closely at the foreign currency. I'd made a chart of the equivalents for easy reference and put it in my wallet. My feelings of disorientation and inadequacy lessened, and I'd felt more like a whole, grown-up person, and less like the new child in school.

I'd been near tears out of frustration with the language and not knowing how to take care of anything, how to find my way around, having to depend so entirely on my husband. And there'd been a quarrel, over nothing—well, it had been something, to me; I'd wanted to eat a piece of salami before we got home and he hadn't wanted to open the white paper wrapping. But quarreling only separated, hardened, and diminished us, and made my daughter silent. Shouldn't a quarrel be about something bigger, to merit the consequence of distance from my husband and my daughter?

The next day my daughter and I went with a woman whose husband, too, was teaching at the conference, and her year-old baby. We had lunch on a small terrace next to a little park. There were peach damask tablecloths overlaid on white cloths, green bottles of cold sparkling water, potatoes with fresh rosemary, melon and prosciutto, grilled chicken, salad, crème caramel, cappuccino. To let my friend finish eating, when the baby had begun to fuss, I'd taken him in my arms and walked him up and down, nibbling on his toes lined up on each foot like a row of tiny pink balloons. In this foreign country, the baby and I were alike; every single sight, sound, and smell was new and fascinating, yet we were unskilled, unable to navigate or speak the language, were dependent on others. But when I held the baby, his head a warm sweet fruit against my cheek as I fed him pink watermelon, I murmured in his ear words of a language I had mastered long ago—the Mother Song; sounds of comfort.

Later, my daughter and I took an afternoon nap, the "riposo," and were wakened several hours later by church bells, ringing dozens of times, in a dolorous duet. My head ached. When my husband returned, we all went to a cafe for tuna-and-artichoke sandwiches on soft white crustless bread, gelati, and lemon soda. My daughter wanted to stay out later, and we quarreled. I was already irritated because she'd moved my clean underpants and bra before they were dry and left wet towels on the floor. She said, petulantly, "Do you have PMS?" Back in the apartment again, I said to her, "I'd like to cease all human interaction now."

My husband was to give a reading of his work on Monday. On Sunday, as I was trying to order food at a restaurant, he corrected my Italian. When the waiter left the table I turned to him coldly and said—sticking a pin of words into him—"Maybe you should spend the next years being sweet while I correct everything you say and do."

And later, as we left the apartment, I realized I had left the one-and-only key inside, even though my husband had asked me if I was sure I had it. My daughter laughed. The only way to get the key was to call the fire department to send someone to crawl through the window, and although I protested that I would take care of it, my husband pointed out that my Italian was not sufficient, and carried the problem away by himself, like a dog with a bone.

The fire department sent three young men, as handsome as if they had been cast in an Italian movie, who were happy to show off in front of my daughter. But later, as I sat in the audience applauding my husband, and he smiled at me, I wanted the trip to be over. The light in Italy revealed too much.

But that moment passed, and we went by car with a group to a small forest that people believe to be sacred. There was an old hotel with an outdoor fire, and a big comfortable table under the sky. Our friend made us laugh until we cried. My husband rubbed my shoulders to help my headache. There were mushrooms, beans in oil, a roasted chicken, the scent of rosemary. The stars were brilliant in the dark sky, and after this late dinner, as we passed under the ancient trees, my husband slid his arm around my waist, and I turned to him, asked, "May I have a sacred kiss in this sacred wood?"

Episode 16

Picking Up the Stitches I Dropped

Snow again, last night, and the branches of the lilac bushes are all edged with white against their black delicacy. The roof of the house behind us has a perfect cap of snow—the telephone and electric wires, too. The birds are quick and darting in the still yard—a cardinal's bright red is a cheerful shock of color.

This is my daughter's last school year at home. She will be leaving for college in the fall. The other day I was walking by an office building that has a daycare center on the first floor, with floor-to-ceiling windows, and the blinds open, and I saw a little girl, about two, with a lock of hair sticking out from her barrette, who looked just like my daughter used to look. The Vietnamese Buddhist monk Thich Nhat Hanh, whose books I so admire, writes "Celebrate impermanence!" because, of course, if things didn't change, children would never grow up, our lives would not progress, and yet . . . I can't help longing for the past, at times.

As I walked along in the sunlight, I thought of my daughter at daycare long ago, of my son at a daycare back in Vermont when I was a single mother—the road up to his daycare was bumpy, and each morning when I drove him there before I went to my job as a secretary, I would sing, only jokingly, "We will never, ever, meet again on the bumpy road to love," but at that time I had no idea how fast all of those ordinary days would pass.

⌐

I have been providing social work services to the patients of an oncologist, and I made a hospital visit today to a woman, a poor fellow creature imprisoned in her body, and until later—after I saw how a pain pill smoothed out her face, and even, by the time I left, brought a smile—I hadn't realized how wild her face had looked when I first arrived, like that of a horse thrashing in its stall.

Desperate to talk despite the effort it cost her, she had begun at once, as soon as I crossed the threshold. In a hoarse whisper, hard for me to hear, she began, "Don't you think it's terrible to have to be like this?" And she seemed relieved when I at once replied, "Yes, I do. It must be really terrible for you."

She can move her head back and forth, and talk, but she's paralyzed and incontinent, has to be fed and toileted, has spent the past few years in bed, and now tumors have spread so that she is swollen all around her head. Her ears have been grotesquely squashed.

"Do you know what it's like to sit in blood?" she asked. She told me of being left unattended during her menstrual period in another facility. "It was like being in prison!" she said. At night there, she felt totally cut off from the world. So she got out, against medical advice, but her husband blamed this decision for her lack of progress. She was troubled by the worry that her daughter, a young adult, still needed her and she must try to stay alive for her. Yet she told me what it was like for her to fall asleep and keep waking up to this same intolerable physical condition.

I asked her if she wanted her family to let her go and she answered, "I'm not sure." I asked her if I might touch her arm for a moment as I sat by her bed and she nodded and then told me a long story of how she tried to tell her husband that to her, being touched was more an expression of love than was sex. She said, "When someone touches you, it shows they really care."

Her pain had increased, though, and her cruel itching had begun. I called in the nurse, who gave her water with a straw and lots of pills. But a few minutes later she suddenly began to cough —I moved away as she said she was going to throw up, and I stepped outside the room to call the nurse. This poor soul vomited, unable to turn over, and had a bowel movement at the same time. A crew of two women aides cleaned her up, and after a bit I was allowed back in. She hadn't thrown up her pain pill —I checked that with the nurse—so when I returned she was calm; she even smiled at me. All the time she talked she'd kept saying my name, as if invoking a spirit.

⌣

Growing up, I got little if any encouragement to use my talents in the "outer" world. The outer world belonged to others, almost entirely men, so far as I could see, so, like many women, I made the most I could of the "inner" world. The work of caring for others' bodies is mainly done by women, who work as nurses and nurses' aides in hospitals and nursing homes.

Even in my writing, which, aside from my diaries, has largely been about the needs of children and women, my primary focus has been caring for others. I value my work in human terms, but it is not valuable to the society in monetary terms. Despite the obvious value to others of my work as a therapist, after more than a decade I am wondering if it is good for me to be so immersed in others' troubles. As a mother, I have been caring for my children for over a quarter of a century, and I am nearing a time when I need to be caring more for myself.

But during this precious last year when my daughter is still at home I am grateful to be able to care for her. She'd asked plaintively, "Are you going to be home tomorrow?" And had turned down a babysitting job, saying "I want to spend the day with Mom." So we went to the pancake house, where, every so often while she has been in high school, we would have a special breakfast on a "hooky day." Then we stopped at the car dealership to have a wobble fixed (a bad tire, it turned out) and browsed in the showroom while they fixed it. I pretended I'd buy her a car. "Which one would you like, dear?" She dreamed back, "The black Mustang convertible."

Then we went to actually buy her something: three bras at Victoria's Secret. When I was her age, "nice" girls wore only plain cotton underpants and bras. I'd only heard whispers about something called the Frederick's of Hollywood catalogue, but never seen it, and now, everyone's daughter wears the kind of sexy underwear that was only hidden in plain brown wrappers in my day. My daughter and I strolled about the mall with our arms linked, laughing a lot.

Before she went out that evening she stopped in my study. "I love you so much," she said, "I don't know what I'd do without you."

I put my arms around her. "You'd manage," I said. "By that time you'll have a family of your own."

"I know," she said, "but I'd be so sad, forever."

"When I was your age," I said, (those immortal Mother-Words) "I had only a few more years of my mother. But I don't smoke anymore, I don't drink, I take good care of myself. I hope to be around for a long, long, time."

In the car, earlier, after we'd gotten her new glasses frames, she'd thanked me, saying, "Thanks, Mommy! You're such a good mother." I'd looked at her, pleased but a bit skeptical of the praise; quizzical. "You know that, don't you?" she said. "You're the best." I would hold those loving words close to me, I would need to remember she'd said them, felt them, when, some years later, she was going through a period of telling me everything I had ever done wrong.

I dreamt that I dropped, upside down, a leather carrying-case full of precious jewelry inside a jewelry store. I wasn't sure I even knew all of what had been in the case and therefore what now was lost, stolen, or ruined, as there was no control over who was coming and going in the store, and were they even looking where they were stepping? I think most of the jewelry was fragile or broken, but I wanted to save it so I could reset it. I guessed I'd never recover what I had spilled.

I sat in her room as she packed, and I'd already begun getting the great pile of laundry ready; all the bedding for the peculiarly student-sized dormitory bed, the towels, the plastic carry-all for the communal bathroom. My daughter is leaving, never to live at home again, only home for at least a few summers (I hope) and visits.

We took her to college in New York City. All of it was awful, for me. My husband and I quarreled about how to get her there. He wanted to drive, but riding in the car makes me so anxious, I wanted to fly, and we did fly, and got a hotel room in order to get her set up at school, but we quarreled there, too.

Much of it was our nerves—we were nervous and unsettled about having to let her go. At the high iron gate of her campus, I made a joke that wasn't really a joke and held on to her, saying "I won't let you go!" as she laughed and pulled away. About half an hour after we'd said goodbye, we were sitting, gloomy, in a restaurant near the campus, and we saw her striding right by on the sidewalk, seeming excited. We turned and just looked at each other.

In my favorite coffee shop at home, days later, having left my once-upon-a-time baby at college in New York City—in that giant, noisy, incomprehensible, far-away place—I suddenly buried my face in my hands because I missed her bright presence and our laughing. I felt as I imagine I would feel after major surgery.

After she called, a few days later, missing us, I came upstairs, to what had been her room, and instead of feeling full of our new life, the upstairs felt only empty of the old, which I wanted back. Downstairs, I missed hearing the sound of her feet (her very weight) moving overhead. I tried to understand that a daughter needs to get away from her mother. In my social-work education and training, I of course learned about the stages of human development. But it's not what I ever felt as a daughter. I never had enough of my mother to want to get away from her. She nearly died my first year at college, and was sick from then on. And then did die, when I was twenty-eight. I always wished I'd had more of her, not less.

Having coffee upstairs in my study, stirring that brown, large-crystal sugar that we had in Italy into the delicate china-cup-with-a-bird-painted-on-it that my husband had given me, I heard the sounds of kids on their way to school, and felt a big pang for my daughter, for the past. When she was home, my life —so much of it—had been centered around her—what she did, how she was, where she was—and even when she was old enough to be left alone, even after she was out much of the time. Despite my jobs, my writing, our trips, she remained a center. I couldn't just hunker down within myself, think about how I was, how I felt. This blessing of privacy and freedom came at the cost of missing her.

But I reminded myself it was time for her to be gone. We had experienced the seventeen years of home and school with her: the friends over for the night, the PTA, the science fairs, the school conferences, the bikes, the ice-skating lessons, the lipstick in junior high, the first year of high school, and the last. The metamorphosis from gap-toothed girl in Smurf glasses to young woman.

Now it was someone else's time for that, and our time for this. So, this childless morning, this Monday, as other mothers' children returned to school and I heard their voices outside the window, I rose at my own time, made a pot of tea to put on a tray, and turned my attention away from those years of nurturing children, to the new and exciting task of nurturing another young girl from the past—myself—who, at ten and twelve would draw and paint, create poems and stories. I'm going back to her, to pick up the stitches I dropped.

The House at Ellison Bay

Episode 17

Up North

I don't know, or need to know, what time it is, these long, clockless days up here in Ellison Bay. I have stopped doing social work, having decided that I needed to take more time for myself and having begun to write picture books for young children — books that I wish my mother could have had as a child; that I could have had. I have closed my office, and my husband has several weeks until he begins teaching again, so we came up here just as all the vacationers were heading back home. I had the most wonderful feeling of escaping, of heading toward a retreat, as we were driving north on the peninsula, past all the cars in the clogged lanes heading south, ending their vacations.

This is the first September of my life that I have not had to return to school or a job, and the first September in twenty-six years that I haven't had a child at home who is beginning the school year.

We wake early (the birds, the open window shades) then fall asleep again in our peaceful upstairs bower. It is so quiet. I come downstairs and have coffee on the back stoop listening to the

139

birds. The mourning dove coos. A quick-moving, ground-feeding blackbird hops about under the willow.

It's some years now that I've been reading books by the Buddhist monk Thich Nhat Hanh, and meditating. (The bookstore clerk, when he added up my stack of books, teased, "That's a lot of enlightenment!")

Sitting on the back stoop of our cottage, I see that, like the trees, I am just another form of life, that all life is made from different combinations of the same elements. Yet a willow is not a maple or a pine. Each is a different manifestation of life. Unlike a human being, though, the willow has no brain to inform it of its existence, nor a heart to grow fond of others and feel pain at their pain, or at their absence.

The willow and the maple and the pine have cast their seeds effortlessly and now there is a new small forest growing in our backyard. And I cast my son, my daughter—growing, still, but far away from me now, in their own lives. Willow, maple, pine, me.

Last night after supper we walked to the shore at Cedar Grove. The water was completely still—I don't remember ever seeing it that still: a mirror to the sky, which was apricot and violet blue. The colors, the satiny look on the still water, and the thin, white line of the horizon made me nearly dizzy—as my husband put it, it was like looking at infinity. A lone duck paddled through the violet blue and apricot satin, leaving a perfectly even wake, and quacking occasionally.

I keep thinking about bears. The paper said there's a black bear here in Ellison Bay that came over from the Upper Peninsula of Michigan, and last week to Sister Bay. It cleans out birdfeeders. Black bears are not supposed to be so dangerous, but still . . .

Last night when it was so hot, and I couldn't sleep, and came down to the sofa, I thought about our open back door and the smelly garbage just inside it—and me, lying on the sofa. About the bear show we saw on TV and how unpredictable bears are and the scenes of them attacking people in places that had always been considered safe.

A three-hundred-pound bear could go through our screen door in a flash; even our big door is flimsy. This bear hasn't been going in anyone's house or garbage, yet. But, clearly, keeping smelly garbage within scent of it is like an invitation. It's changed the way I feel about the screen door at night, that's for sure. A bear. "Imagine!" as my ten-year-old mother wrote in one of the diaries that I'd found in a box in the basement at home; one diary when she was ten, and two more when she was fourteen and sixteen. Not all the pages were used, but there are enough entries from each period of her life to give me a look into what her life was like, what she thought about.

For the past few years, I have been writing my book about Mother, trying to find out what happened in her life that caused this once lovely, intelligent, talented girl, whose voice I hear in those old diaries, to have ended up as she did. Being unable to help herself get well, to help herself be happy, to help me grow up. I want to understand. These first weeks of freedom, from work, from child-rearing, up here in Wisconsin, I have all day every day to work on it.

In the early morning, I opened the back door abruptly to sit on the stoop in my purple bathrobe with my coffee, and surprised a gray fox, who turned to look at me for quite a long moment before trotting to the back of the yard, then turning to look at me again before disappearing.

"Oh!" I said, startled, and came back inside the door for a moment. Then I came out and reclaimed my spot as homo sapiens. I realize when we see animals in "our" yard that it is our tenure here, not theirs, that is the unexpected one. The creatures that live in this piece of land are startled to see me here.

If the fox were writing a diary, he'd write: "Just as I was heading for home on Garrett Bay Road, a large pale creature, purple with dark hair on its head, appeared and made a short sound. We looked at each other briefly. I could see it was frightened of me, so I trotted on to the back of the yard and onto my path home. I had to turn and look once more, though, for it was standing at the entrance to its nest, still looking at me. It had no tail, or ears!

Early, overcast, rainy in fact. Still. My husband woke me inadvertently by his effort to get dressed. The closet door squeaked, the drawer groaned—we are like one living organism anyway, with one's actions, moods, pains, affecting the other. I could feel I wouldn't be able to return to sleep, but it was okay.

He joined me for my walk up the road that goes past the cemetery. The dew was heavy, left by the fog, and my shoes got wet when I set upright a vase of roses that had fallen over on a recent grave, the bare earth coffin-sized.

We kept on walking, to that road where a barking dog sometimes has sent us away, and then to Town Beach, where we sat on the dock, the fresh, nearly cold breeze on our faces, the warm sun, out now briefly, on our shoulders. The wind made waves and a loud surf over the many shoreline boulders. The water is clear—all of it is still unspoiled: the bluff, the little harbors to our right, the blue water to the horizon.

We meditated sitting on the dock. Then I said, while sitting cross-legged, "I'm interested in meditating, in enlightenment, in writing something beautiful—and in those home-made doughnuts at the diner."

Later, we got sandwiches at the tidy, clean, Fish Creek store, and took them with us to the little park. Gulls begged and harassed us. We read, then took a drive on a meandering road with stone walls, tall cedars, and surprising big mansions overlooking the water. My favorite house, however, is the small one by the park, right downtown, an old house whose windows look out on the bay.

We parked and read again, waiting for my meeting. It got dark, and the lights came on, and someone went into the dollhouse Gibraltar Town Hall to get the coffee ready, and its lights came on. Eight of us at the AA meeting. The nourishment of honest talk and stories of recovery.

A light rain, and in our car, my husband waiting for me, reading by the dome light. A soft-dark ride home up the peninsula, and past a dead deer. The peninsula feels different now, in autumn, than it does in high summer.

⌒

Prior to an afternoon nap, I'd been reading Mother's diary from 1925 when she was fourteen:

> Thursday—Dear, dear, I fear I'm becoming very lax about writing in this worthy (?) document (or what you will). Well, I got sent to the office today from Miss Winter's class. G. DeLong and I were changing slippers—I went and saw Mr. Rae 6th period—he was busy 2nd—and he was awfully nice—but my voice was trembly and shaky and I was scared to death for fear I'd cry. Mother, of course, had spasms. Tonite [sic] the Cabinet played the faculty and we beat 'em about 20 some to 0. Lotsa fun! Our GAA [Girls Athletic Association] pins came today and they are darling!

And from 1927 when she was sixteen:

> Well—caught up at last! I'm getting to bed early tonite—thank heaven! Cabinet meeting this noon and plans for the Competitive vaudeville—a Dutch scene—very fascinating—stayed home tonite to work on Cicero scrapbook—I'm reading a fascinating book —"The White Monkey"!—much sophistication! I love you darling, always!!! [her boyfriend at that time.]

Besides reading the diaries, I'd been looking at the blueprints and photos of the house Mother grew up in, and during my nap I dreamt she was in a compartment on a train that I, too, was on.

"Why, haven't I told you what I'm doing?" I ask her in astonishment, both hands on the sides of my face. "I am writing a book about—well, it's about you, actually, and I'm using your diaries. I mean, I guess I need to ask you, may I use your diaries? And oh, there's so much I would love to talk to you about!"

I was aware of a familiar anxiety that she would not really be interested. "Of course," I say, with growing excitement, "you know absolutely everything that I want to ask—about your father and your mother and your house—about your life." She's not looking into my eyes, as was usually true, in real life.

"Oh, where to begin!" I go on. "We can have lunch together, and talk about it." I rush off to get all my papers together, as I can't go with her until I get all of that important stuff, I can't just leave it—but where is it? How do I get back to my space, and then find hers again? I am suddenly in a seat with my brother on my left and my sister on my right, and we're traveling forward.

"Are we moving?" I ask in great alarm. "Is the train moving forward?" They nod.

"No!" I cry, "Did Mommy get off?"

"Yes," they say, "at that stop back behind us."

I'm frantic, crying, I long so to be with her, we were going to have a meal together, and talk about everything—but she's gotten off, and I couldn't get off, yet, and she is too far back now for me to find her again.

"No, No!" I cry, "I want to be with Mommy!"

I wake feeling I might actually throw up, so full of sadness, frustration, and a terrible longing I remember having felt from a childhood time when she'd driven off to the store without me and I had thought she would wait for me.

Awake, crying, I go downstairs to the empty, clean, sunny, quiet kitchen, aware that I have somehow been returned to this present from the past, to my husband, who says, "I hope writing this book will exorcise this sorrow for you," and holds me. In a while I calm down and we have tea.

⌒

Finally, after days, weeks, months, after, in fact, years, I have finished a draft of my memoir about Mother. When I bundle the whole manuscript into a cardboard box and carry it to my husband to show it to him, I realize that it feels as if I am carrying her cremated remains.

⌣

I am up very early, writing in my little room in our cottage in Ellison Bay, the room with its water heater where once the boy-cat sat with his tail wrapped around his neat paws. I am thinking of the jays' nest my husband took out of our backyard, after they had built it in the spring and have since abandoned it.

It is a marvel. Woven together in the central part with smaller sticks, while larger and coarser sticks make up the outer part, it's practically braided. It must have taken them a long time to build it.

This is a brand-new day. All for me, and for my husband, together up here. I am no longer the youngest child of a depressed and ill mother, no longer a mother raising children, myself, or a wife to that ex-husband who could not see me. My heart no longer needs to ache for my social work clients.

I am free and my own. My time—those irreplaceable hours that make up my life—belongs only to me. I am the whole person I came into this world to be, free to enjoy the beauties and pleasures of life, one day at a time.

I am sober, I am free of addictions. I am a recovering person, able to utilize and appreciate AA, all that was the beginning and key to my path to health, and I have the teachings of Thich Nhat Hanh to aspire to—to work towards. I am grateful for my sobriety. For my husband's love. For my son and my daughter in the world. For this beautiful, peaceful place. If I had remained in that self-made prison of alcoholism and of addiction to cigarettes, every day I would have been destroying myself and destroying my loved ones' possibilities.

How is it that I have been freed from that prison? It is because of human generosity, and because I sought help. Because, so many years ago, now, my best friend referred me to the alcohol counselor, and I went to meet with her. Because that counselor who became my sponsor listened and confirmed the truth about my drinking and talked with me and gave me books to read and took me to AA. Because AA was there. Because I believed what they told me, and I went to meetings, and listened, and learned, and didn't drink, one day at a time. Each thing led to another thing. That's how that jays' nest in our yard got made, one twig at a time. And all this river of time later, here I am, awake in the early morning in Wisconsin—calm, strong, well, full of so much I want to do.

⌐

I began writing here before dawn. Now it's light, and the rest of the world—the up-here world—will wake and stir. A few cars will begin to crawl into the post office lot across from our cottage as village folks stop to check for mail. The yellow school bus will stop, lights flashing, for the little yellow-haired boys across the road. I'll close this diary and begin this day.

Episode 18

The Mother Song

FROM MY DIARY:

I'm sitting at my daughter's desk in her college dorm room. Her September desk pad calendar, marked with her neat, artistic printing in black ink reads, "Mom comes to New York City!" on the seventh and "School starts" on the fifth and "library books due" on the fifteenth.

What a grand dorm apartment she and her two roommates have: French doors onto their balcony and a view there, if you craned your neck, almost into a park—a Parisian feel. She's well aware it's undoubtedly the best place she'll ever be privileged to inhabit in New York City.

A cup of tea, this sunny room, the silence of the sleeping girls—I mean young women—elsewhere in the apartment, and two doses of acetaminophen have made me feel better. I'd waked at four, headachy, in the bed my daughter had given up for me. Her room was still quite a mess, as she was only just getting settled. The apartment is really wonderful for these young women's purposes. Its only disadvantage is that long, dark, railway hall, but, there, at the end of it, in my daughter's room, the sun pours in.

I am in a strange world, yet it is my daughter's. I had said to her after my very first visit to her college three years earlier, "Imagine that you came to see me, but I was in a new place, surrounded by people you didn't know, with a life you had no part of!" That was how I had felt three years ago, an *outsider* to the one who had grown *inside* me. But, happily, this was not that first year's first visit.

My daughter and I had taken the subway here from my son's place in Brooklyn. He has been on his own for long enough that I was mostly more used to seeing him only occasionally and to his having a life that I was not part of.

Once, at home, the phone rang and a man's voice I didn't recognize said hello and I asked who it was. The man said, "Remember a hot day in August, a lot of pain, and then a burst of new life?" And I'd laughed—Oh! My *son*!

I dreamt recently of my son at about four or five years old. I was carrying him on my hip, though he was too big for that, across an icy spot. A man offered to help and said, "Why must you carry him yourself?" I said I was afraid if someone else did they might slip, whereas I was less afraid that I would. I put my son down and he made his way some distance and I couldn't always see him, but then he came out into the open. I called him, and he looked up and smiled and came toward me. I remembered that linking and un-linking of young motherhood, the letting-go and reuniting, the deep connection that ensured he'd come when I called; his smile, our pleasure at our reunion.

In waking life, the reunion with my grown son, and nearly-grown daughter, unsettles me, because it opens doors which I'd had to close—all the old deep inter-relating; my shrinking as a person in my own life and the return of myself as Mother. My daughter still sometimes cuddles up to me, mostly a matter of head-nuzzling and her arms, because the rest of her is too grown, and I'll kiss her cheek with a mother's hungry kiss because this young woman has the child in her. She wants me to recognize and love the child in her, yet also to let go of that child and recognize the woman in her.

Sometimes when I wake in the wee hours I worry about my son's safety, about my daughter's—their Away Lives—so far, so distant from me, in the black night; our mutual life over, closed.

Motherhood is like a dance constantly requiring new steps without enough time to learn them, or a song for which you're always needing to learn new words. And sharing my children with my two ex-husbands—their fathers—and stepmothers and half-siblings—my children's whole other families—have made it even more complicated.

I dreamt that I had driven a train-load of people home safely through difficult and dangerous territory, but no one acknowledged or thanked me when we reached the end of the journey. They all went their ways and I wandered around, wondering if anyone even knew I had been the engineer. But then I thought: everyone expects the train to get you there safely; it's not something they would think to thank you for.

I never imagined that having your children grow up would be the same deep ache as the end of a love affair. I feel left out. My children are so busy with their lives, as they should be, as I want them to be, and yet. So that, recently, all the way downtown to the opera with my husband, I had wept and spoken of feeling worn down by being a mother, used up and set aside like an old toy.

But the sights of the Great City cheered me, and reminded me of the great Other Life, everything other than children—of my husband's and my life together, apart from them, all the many interesting things to do that don't have anything to do with my children: books, work, classes, friends, happy love, trips, curiosity, accomplishments, things to write and read. And in the magnificent opera house with its gorgeous Art Deco lamps and golden ceilings, we had a cup of cappuccino on a chilly night and shared a fat cookie. I don't really like opera, except for *La Bohème*—the stories seem cartoonish and sexist; the women always lose; but I like my husband's pleasure in the music, and his warm hand in the dark.

151

At home, the next evening, the leaves were mostly down in our front yard, those same yellow leaves that marked all the autumns of my children's school years. The light in our bedroom was yellow from the leaves outside.

When my son left for college, and then, some years later, my daughter left, I always had the feeling of an undercurrent of loss, of their absence. But I got (mostly) used to it, and it even came to seem long ago that they had ever lived here.

The green curtains in our bedroom dim the room so pleasantly; fresh air billows them slightly. The sound of children playing in the neighborhood drifts in, comforting and faint. Beyond our bedroom door our house stands empty and private, lamps burning in our rooms.

Graham Greene, in his novel *Our Man in Havana*, says to someone who is grieving, "You were interested in a person, not in life, and people die, or leave us, but if you are interested in life, it never lets you down."

We went for a stroll in our darkening neighborhood. Our four-year-old neighbor was out, raking with his little rake next to his mother. A boy on a bike was riding round and round. A woman sat on her porch with her cat. A child called his dog. We paused to admire some bittersweet and deep-russet autumn flowers and the little front yards that were carefully tended, and then we ambled along, a middle-aged couple whose children had gone.

Episode 19

I Hope You Find Your Hat

I had left the church where the meeting had been and was riding the city bus past the cemetery that used to be an orchard, and I thought, as I do every single time I pass that cemetery-once-an-orchard, about my daughter's friend's mother who was buried there. About how she must be lying, still, after all these years, in the exact same position her body had been in at the funeral when she'd been laid out for all to see, unmoving. And as I put my hand in my yellow canvas bag, the one that hangs so handily across my body so that I could just stuff things in it—a book, a scarf, gloves, a hat—I realized that my hat was not in there.

⌣

I had taken the hat out of the closet that morning, the first spring-like day—if you can call it spring-like when some snow was still, in places, piled in dirty clumps on the sides of the street. I had taken the hat out of the closet because the sun was so bright, and the hat had a brim just wide enough to protect my face, and my face, since I hadn't taken enough care about it when I was young, was now prone to pre-cancer spots and I'd even had one actual cancer—easily enough removed, after all, but still. Having nearly forgotten the hat, which I'd bought only last spring, I felt happy to see it again, to be able to wear it, because it really was a perfect hat for me—lightweight, cotton, easy to stuff quickly into that yellow canvas bag or even a coat pocket, yet it protected my face, and was, though not exactly fashionable, not actually awful as a lot of hats are; as, in fact, most hats are.

I'd clapped it onto my head early that morning as I left our apartment to take a quick walk around the block, past the white clapboard church with the blue door and the sign reading "God is Still Speaking," and I'd muttered, under my breath, "Well, good luck with that!"

I'd taken just a very short walk before my friend was to pick me up for the meeting we were going to, the twelve-step meeting where I was still learning how powerless I am over other people, and often, powerless even over my own feelings, but I was also reminded that I at least have power over my own actions.

⌐

I'd needed to walk. My back had been aching, partly from not walking enough, and that nerve in my left thigh had been acting up, that nerve that gave me unpredictable shocks like I imagined an electric prod would feel. And I needed the hat to keep that sun, warm and lovely though it was, from my face— those spots the doctor called "pre-cancer," like, I thought, life could be called "pre-death."

I was happy, walking in the sun yet protected from its harmful rays, happy that it was, finally, after an unusually cold winter, and what the weather report calls a polar vortex—a period of time in which the cold and ice, instead of moving on, just stayed put, and caused the world beneath to shiver—it was finally almost spring. And for the past few years, I'd been under another kind of polar vortex, a coldness between my son and me that wouldn't move on and beneath which I, and I imagined that he, too, shivered.

I was happy, as I walked, that I was about to see my friend, because we always laughed about things that would, in other circumstances, make you cry, and when, as I came around the corner by my building, I saw her car at the curb, I quickened my pace. As I approached the car I could see my friend bent over her phone, texting, and I leaned down to knock on the window. She looked up and made a gesture of surprise, unlocked the door so I could get in, and we both laughed, because she'd just been texting me that she was early.

And this turned out to be the last moment when I remembered having my hat.

⌐

When we'd parked at the curb near the yellow brick church for the meeting, I'd had to wait for my friend to get out and then I'd had to crawl across the driver's seat to get out myself, because there was a chunk of snow keeping the passenger door from opening. Maybe I'd dropped my hat on the pavement still covered in spots with crusty, dirty snow, and walked away, not noticing?

Later, I called the church office. The woman in the office was as nice and sympathetic as you would think someone who works in a church office would be. She took down my phone number and promptly called back to say she'd gone downstairs to the room where we'd had our meeting, and checked the stairs, but found no hat. She would keep my number and call me if anyone turned it in.

Maybe, just maybe—though I didn't think so—I'd left it in the restaurant where my friend had dropped me after the meeting but before I took the bus. I'd had a cup of tea and a bite and read my book by Anthony Trollope, the third one of his I'd read in a row. I'd hit the jackpot with Trollope, he'd written so many books—forty-seven novels!—that I'd have a lot of reading pleasure ahead. His stories of people's relationships comforted me. There was, really, no difference at all between my own difficulties and the difficulties of people Trollope portrayed more than a hundred and fifty years ago.

There were differences, certainly, in customs between Victorian England and post-9/11 America; certainly not the same weather terms as "polar vortex," but no difference at all in the ways people loved, sorrowed, struggled, suffered, were estranged or were dear to one another. Henry James said of Trollope that he "helped the heart of man to know itself" (The heart of woman, too, Mr. James). Our difficulties had always been so, were still so, and would continue to be so, if, that is, the world continued, which did not always seem likely.

I sometimes stopped reading the news. If only everyone really cared about each other, the worst problems could be solved. But it was sad and obvious truth that some people in the world, like me, could have enough to eat, could sleep in a warm apartment, while, elsewhere, people went hungry, or slept on the streets, or in tents in camps.

I could have a nice hat, and some people had no hat at all. I tried to even the score a little by donating money every month to certain groups doing good, but there was no way to even the score; it was blind luck that I was born into having what I had.

I called the cafe but it was closed, and there was no way to leave a message. So I could still hope that my hat might be there, though I didn't think it was.

I decided to take another bus back to the yellow brick church where the meeting had been. I no longer had a car, hadn't driven for more than a decade, not since we'd moved to the apartment after selling the house in which my son and daughter had grown up. We could walk to just about everything, and there were buses, cabs, and trains for anything we couldn't walk to. I'd discovered I liked not owning a car, that it offered a freedom like that of not owning a dog that you had to walk, and clean up after, and take to the vet.

As I waited at the bus stop, a cab approached, so I hailed it, thinking it would be a faster way to get back to the church in case my hat might still be lying in the street or sidewalks near it. "I need for you to take me back to a place where I think I lost my hat," I told the driver after I got in the cab and gave him directions.

He was middle-aged—at least I thought so, from what I could see of him from the back seat of the cab, and he spoke with a foreign accent. As he drove, we talked of the weather, the cold winter, the polar vortex, and he said how it was hard to drive a cab in the winter, because not only was it cold, but it was dark, and when it was dark, it was more dangerous. A cabbie had recently been shot, he told me, and another cabbie, stabbed. There were areas of the city so dangerous that he, and other drivers, too, he said, when they saw the address, were not willing to go there.

I asked why the cab didn't have a protective wall between him and his passengers, like the cabs in New York City, but he said a lot of drivers didn't like them because they cramped the driver's seat, and that he never knew what car he would get, anyway, so one car might have that protection and another might not.

"Would it be at all possible for you to get another job?" I asked, aware, though, that the economy was terrible, that so many people worked for wages that would not support them, and that they could not afford or sometimes even obtain medical insurance.

"Well, not really," he replied, "because the only job I could get is minimum wage, and then you have to work two or three jobs just to get by."

"Oh," I said. "Of course. I see. I'm sorry. That is hard." There was a brief silence.

"Well," I said, "I guess maybe we should talk about something more cheerful."

"Yes," he agreed. "Let's talk about spring, and how soon where we now see snow there will be beautiful green grass. Look!" he said, pointing out a large patch of grass showing beneath melted snow. "There's green grass already, see?"

"I do see it," I said. "Isn't that great! Grass!"

"My sister," he said, "wants me to move to Arizona where she lives. And where my nieces and nephews are. I live by myself here, and I like it here, but it's not so good to not have family—

if I was sick, no one would even know, but if I was in Arizona my sister would look in on me two or three times a day. But it is so hot there."

"Well, it is hot there," I agreed. "But it seems like it would be really nice to be near your family."

How I wished I could live close to my son, to my daughter, to my grandchildren, how I shared the cab driver's wish to be cared for by family, though, of course, luckily, I had my husband, still, who does care for me; who loves me, and whom I love, though I don't say it that way, don't say, as I've heard other older women say, since many of their friends are widows, "I still have my husband."

We arrived back at the church. "I'm just going to jump out and look up and down the street where we parked," I said.

"Do you want me to help you look?" the cab driver asked.

"Thanks, but no," I replied. "If you don't mind waiting just a minute, I will take a look."

I walked as quickly as I could, careful not to slip and fall—another thing older women often talk about, the danger, to our older bones, of falling—up and down the crusty snow on the side of the street where my friend had parked. I could see that my hat was not there, was not on the edges of the shoveled walk to the church, was nowhere.

"Nope. No hat," I said, getting back in the cab, then telling him my address.

After we had driven a few miles, the driver said, "This is a dangerous neighborhood." We were by the high school where my son and daughter had gone, many years earlier. It was awfully hard to stop, I thought, the way a mother is expected to stop, after all the years of taking care of children, of loving them. How can a mother be expected to just stop wanting to be important to them? Such a passion, this mothering, that is forced to become a cool, detached thing. Of course I know that children grow up, live elsewhere, have lives of their own. I know that all I could expect was to be a part of their lives, but it seemed I had become such a very small part.

The neighborhood was dangerous, at times, I agreed with the cab driver. I told him it was true, there had been a shooting once, it was after my own children had graduated, luckily—a high school student had died, right on this street, right where that streetlight was. I remembered the spot distinctly, remembered driving by it when there had been flowers left there.

"That's terrible," he said.

We rode another mile in silence, and then the driver pulled his cab up to our apartment building. I paid the fare, and gave him what I hoped he found to be a generous tip, and got out of the cab. As I closed the door, he leaned into the open window on the curb side of the cab and said, "I hope you find your hat!"

Episode 20

Many Lamps

One October, five years after my daughter graduated from college, too early in the morning to possibly be good news, she telephoned me. "Mom! Dad *died!*"

At once I was remembering my ex-husband, her father, resting his hand on my shoulder for a moment at my son's wedding as we'd stood looking together at the amusing and clever organizational chart that my daughter—our daughter—had drawn so that the wedding guests could understand who had been married to whom and whose children were whose in our complicated extended family. It was the only time he had touched me since I had left him when my daughter was two-and-a half.

I was remembering the wide, smooth expanse of his strong chest as a young man, his golden hair, how white the whites of his blue eyes had been—our brief happiness, our daughter's birth.

In New Hampshire, on the day of his funeral, I woke to tears from a dream that he was getting out of a bath or shower. I saw that broad chest and back and said, "Oh! You moved! You got up! You're not really lying in that coffin!" I stumbled up out of bed, aware it was light, aware it was raining, chilly, mournful weather outside.

I went into the hotel bathroom to take off my nightgown and I saw my naked body in the mirror and cried, remembering our two living bodies, so long ago, and how he'd looked in his coffin the night before—like a wooden cigar store mannequin, his brow, his nose, his face painted, his once-golden hair dull, dry; he looked like my ex-husband, only dead, only dead, only dead.

All the memories had been let out and were flying about, and I grieved for that sad marriage and divorce and for whatever pretty things there had been before the years of ugly things.

Later, I cleaned off from the bottom of my shoes the mud from his grave.

I woke at the house of my son and his wife with an instant knot behind my right eye, as my grandson, their three-year-old, shouted "Daddy!" I went into the hall from the TV room where my husband and I had been sleeping and I said softly outside my grandson's door, "It's not time yet, go back to sleep," and I heard him saying, "Oma? Oma? Oma?"—my preferred term for "grandmother," the word Mother had used with her grandchildren—and to his muted calls I went downstairs to get his milk in his sippy cup, and came back up to see my husband lifting him out of his crib, which looked Lilliputian now, my grandson towered in it, but he wasn't asking yet to have a real bed, and I saw with gladness his lovely, sleepy face.

He and I had a little visit then in the TV room before I later became resigned to turning on the television.

"What did you dream?" I always asked.

He furrowed his brow, thinking. I knew he was making it up for me. He answered after quite a while: "A train!"

"Ah!" I said, then, "I dreamt I gave away a diamond ring!" He looked thoughtfully at me.

I turned on the TV and he lined up on the couch his red bear, baby bunny, and his naked, plastic doll. "He's bald," my grandson explained. He tucked them under the pretty knitted blanket his other grandmother had made for him, and he instructed them about Dino Dan. I did like Dino Dan, the children's show made in Canada. I liked Dan's spacious, comfortable, old-fashioned brick house on a tree-lined open street. The house, a big square one with a nice round attic window, reminded me of one of the houses I had grown up in.

My son's squat, solid little dog, his plastic bone in his mouth, came up and rolled his buggy eyes and made a little grunting noise. He wanted to come up on the sofa, and despite his short legs, he made the leap, then backed up into me in his funny style, to make contact. I was pretty happy watching Dino Dan with my warm grandson and his entourage of stuffed toys on one side, the warm dog on the other. I liked looking at the young strong mother of Dan and thinking about back when I was like her.

Later in the afternoon, I read and sang my grandson to sleep. "I'm 'cited to see you!" he'd said to me when we had first arrived.

"I'm glad!" I'd said. "Because I missed you."

"I missed you too," he'd said, and we'd smiled at one another.

"We're traveling through time together!" I said.

"We are?" he asked.

"Yup!" I replied. "You've been traveling for three years and I've been traveling sixty-five years!"

"You have?" he asked wonderingly.

⌐

Then it was what I thought of as "The Grandmother's Hour," that sleepy afternoon time of little children napping, the dog in, and nothing to do or needing to be done in the outside world. That was fine with me. But how restless it used to make me, as a young mother. I remembered how forlorn and left out of life I sometimes felt when my daughter was small and my son would be coming home from school. I didn't feel cozy or content, because my future ex-husband, who could not see me, was then my husband—and I was lonely and I longed for more Life. Oh, how things changed, and changed again! Now my son was out, living, and I was home with his son, and my ex-husband was dead.

⌣

My daughter and her two-year-old daughter were visiting. My granddaughter wanted to cuddle with me, so she and I settled onto the couch and I read her a little Beatrix Potter book, surprised, when I opened it, to see, written on the front page, my daughter's name, "With love from Gram and Granddaddy" (my ex-husband's parents). My granddaughter pointed to the pictures and said, "Mommy rabbit, Daddy rabbit," then, "Many rabbits." "Many" was her favorite new word, and the night before, in this enchanted time before bed, she'd looked around our living room and said, "Many lamps."

After we'd looked at the book, she kept lying up against me, or stretching out on the couch with her head on my lap, constantly shifting position, saying "Hi Oma," and I'd reply, "Hi, I missed you, I'm so glad to see you!" and I stroked her hair and face. She lay on her belly and put her face practically between my legs, as if sensing the Mother Ship, and said, over and over, "Hi Oma." It's what she could verbalize; I imagined it took the place of "I missed you, I'm happy to be together again, I love you," all of this feeling contained in "Hi Oma." My husband came in the room, smiling, eager to be with us, and sat next to me, then my daughter came in, too, and then her visiting half-sister, my ex-husband's daughter whom I called my "half-daughter," and joined us, and, delighted, we had my granddaughter across our four laps.

My daughter said she needed me all of this hot month of July in New York City and so that is where I was. My back hurt, and I was tired, but I had the beauty of my two-year-old granddaughter, and also of my daughter's belly, rippling with the new baby boy due any day. He was tumbling around inside my daughter last night as together on the sofa we sat watching a documentary about bin Laden, a weird juxtaposition: terrorism, and a new life safe and enclosed.

Big storms were due. "Munder!" said my granddaughter, but the rumbling thunder came to nothing, like my daughter's many pains. That was the feeling of these days, this huge event, the birth, which like a storm was building, rumbling, but not yet arrived. My husband was flying from home in Illinois toward us, and it would be such a help to have him. My daughter and I would be able to complete a sentence, and my husband and granddaughter enjoy each other so much.

In the afternoon, while my granddaughter was asleep, my daughter took me up on my offer to massage her back. Real contractions, three minutes apart, had begun. Earlier, as we were walking back from the park and I was behind her, I'd felt tender and anxious, seeing her waddling, her belly distended like a mare's, and, she'd said, aching from the pressure of this baby.

Because she'd asked, I sat behind her, me on the couch, her on the ottoman in front of me, between my legs, and I rubbed her back and shoulders as we waited for her husband, who was rushing home from work to take her to the hospital. I lifted her heavy, glossy hair from her hot neck. Soon her husband, excited and nervous, arrived, and off they went.

After two days of my husband and me caring for her, and her daddy going back and forth to the hospital, and her visit there to Mama and the new baby, my granddaughter got an intense longing for her mother. She pointed at the green chair where her mama usually sat and cried "Mama! Hold you!" which was her way of saying "Hold me." She began to cry, "Mama, Mama, Mama, hold you!" but I was there to hold her, and then Daddy took her to bed, and the next day Mama and the new baby came home.

From a Letter to My Mother

PART FOUR

In your day, Mother, a woman probably couldn't even think that she might not like or want children. I mean the actual children, not the idea of them. The idea of them is what makes people keep having them, don't you think? Like your mother. Though she stopped after having one—you—as far as I know. She must have loved your father, and wanted to have a child with him, or at least knew that he wanted to have a child and so she needed to have one, for him. But somehow I think—imagine—that she wouldn't have liked things having to do with her body. She was so meticulous, judging from the photos. So concerned with appearances. I would think she would have liked to keep her body to herself, that she would have hated the indignities of giving birth.

But perhaps I'm wildly off. After all, I know her—my own grandmother, whose genes I carry—only through a few brief encounters. Only once, when I was fifteen, was I in that fancy house of hers, a mansion, with you, and I went into her bathroom and bedroom while you and she were out, and I looked in the cupboards and drawers, where I found soaps, lotions, and bottles of her favorite fragrance (gardenia), and silk nightgowns, and white boxes with long, white kid gloves with pearl buttons. We were served meals by her maid at her dining table, lit by silver candelabras; at each place there was a sterling silver ashtray and matching matchbox. All I knew of my grandmother was that one visit, and a box of photographs; some letters to you; some entries in your girlhood diaries. And her possessions, which came to you after she'd died— her mirrors, her silver cigarette case, the green crystal cocktail glasses, the silver jigger made to look like a thimble ("Just a thimbleful" engraved on it—the drinker's rationalization) that were somehow passed on to me.

Maybe she was very sexy. Maybe she had multiple orgasms. Maybe her white gloves, her ladylike dresses, her pearls, covered a voluptuous, pleasure-loving woman. I'll never know.

It's not surprising, really, that I find myself wondering about my grandmother's sexuality. It is through sex that she and I are so intimately related. She had sex with your father and got pregnant with you. Female babies are born with all their eggs, so, in a way, when she gave birth to you, she gave birth to half of me, too: half of me was already in you, as an egg.

What was that labor giving birth to you like, for her, in 1911? Women gave birth at home. Was her mother with her? Or her sister, your beloved aunt, whose name I carry, was she there? I found the newspaper announcement of your birth, Mother, in the *Mason City Globe Gazette*. Someone wrote, "the stork left one of the choicest rosebuds of the season at this home this morning." Your father's smile was described as "unusually large this morning."

But your mother never repeated the experience. Somehow I think it's because she thought once was more than enough. Maybe that's another reason you had so many children. To be different from your mother. You were comfortable and matter-of-fact about labor. You never scared me about it, the way some women seem to like to scare others with their stories. I saw that labor was something a woman faced with equanimity, courage. It never would have occurred to me to scream, though I couldn't help groaning. "It's not like other pain," you told me, "because there's a baby at the end."

Well, it certainly was not like other pain, Mother—it was so much worse than anything I'd yet experienced, and it had an undergirding of plain misery, which I hadn't expected. But, yes, there was a baby at the end. And though I thought, right afterwards, "I don't ever want to go through that again," I did, and it was worth it.

Perhaps, Mother, when I said earlier that I could have more sympathy for those who were handicapped, who didn't have choices, I should have seen that there are handicaps that are invisible to the eye. Though you were educated, privileged, you'd been handicapped by your father's death and by your mother's criticism. You didn't feel lovable. And then my father picked you.

When you were young, you were, as I know so well from your girlhood diaries, in love with the idea of love. You had, like all young people, your romantic notions, your dreams. You thought you had escaped your mother's criticisms. You had left her, and Mason City, Iowa, and the church, and the values you'd been raised with, to be a flapper. It was the nineteen-twenties, and everything was changing. Your mother's Victorian world was over.

What a life you and my father were going to fashion for yourselves! Newly married, you two were living in what my father wrote to his old friend was a "reconditioned whorehouse" in Kansas City. My father was "trying to make a living by the pen" and you wanted to go to art school to learn how to draw cartoons and show you were as witty as Dorothy Parker.

Instead, you had my oldest brother. And then another child, and another, and another, and another, each of us an additional obstacle to that dream of being artists and writers, until—my father never earning enough money, you holding everything together with bubble gum—that obstacle was as impenetrable as a beaver's dam.

But—I haven't been a child for more than half a century. What could be the point of worrying over what kind of parents you and my father were? I guess because those first ten years of life are when the scaffolding of one's personality is set. And one needs to figure out how one has been put together—what one's scaffolding is—in order to be free. To use a different metaphor, in order not to be driven by those underwater currents, but to be free to drive oneself, to be, as the Buddhists say, *aware*.

In your first ten years, Mother—when *your* scaffolding of your personality was being set—your father suddenly died. You and your mother went to live for a while with some relative in Miami Beach. I know this not because you ever told me, but because of the diary you kept for some months that year. In it, you sound lonely, an only child surrounded by adults. Your mother going out a lot to parties and polo matches and society events, not there even the day you had a special program at your school.

173

It seems that part of your scaffolding, erected in those years, was that even when you lost the most precious thing in your life, you had to bear it alone and not make a fuss. Oh, Mother. What a terrible lesson for a little child to learn. Because she can't—you couldn't—bear it alone. It's too much, for a child, even for an adult, to bear it alone. It damages her. It damaged you. You lived through it, yes. You locked it away. But Life added to that first, terrible grief. It always does. With each additional grief, your lock had to grow stronger. And stronger. Locked away, too, with your grief, was your empathy, first for yourself, and later, for your oldest son, being beaten by your husband. And for me, when at thirteen my front tooth was pulled, and you and my father didn't get that gaping hole fixed, and sent me into and through adolescence needing to cover my mouth whenever I smiled.

But let me invite you to make a fuss. Make a fuss! Sit with me at the kitchen table in my house, beneath the Buddha statue at the kitchen altar. Let the tea I've poured for you grow cold, as you pour out your grief to me. Cry—I'll listen, I'll be with you—those tears you didn't, couldn't, cry before; let them pour down your cheeks. Tell me, finally, how it felt to you when your father died. When your oldest son, as a grown man, left his wife and baby and disappeared, went missing for many years. When my father left you in the nursing home and went back to *your* home with his girlfriend, your old friend.

Tell me, if you can talk through your tears, and if you can't, just cry. I'll sit with you. The balm of my attention, will, I promise you, ease your burden. If you cry enough, if you tell enough, your burden, truly, Mother, will be lighter. Because we will share it. Fifty years, sixty years, seventy years—the years make no difference at all, to unspoken grief. It's like that prehistoric man whose body was found frozen in the ice, over 5,000 years old, and still poised to defend himself, the arrows still in his quiver. The hikers who found him thought, at first, that he had recently died. Only, his clothes were like those of a figure in a museum! He had a crude ax, its stone head fastened on with twine!

Time, Mother, is nothing. And everything.

When you've cried enough, and told me all about your sadness, I hope you'll see that, for a while, anyway, it's my turn. I'll make a fresh pot of tea, and pour you a cup. Listen, then, to me, Mother. I'll tell you how I felt when you died. No—those awful years before you died. How it felt, not to be able to save you. How I had to watch you destroy yourself, as if you were lowering yourself, inch by inch, into scalding water.

I'll tell you how I longed for you, my mother, to mother me. How I longed to be the apple of your eye. To have you delighted to see me, to hear about me. To have your guidance, your advice.

I could tell you about my own bad choices. Two divorces. My attempts, like yours, to create a happy, loving family. My depression, that settling on me like pigeons roosting on a roof. Shining through, my two beautiful children. Of finding my husband—his finding me—our love, despite love's imperfections, that's lasted. The years of life together, the times we managed to be a happy, loving family. The pain my children had to endure, the losses they had to suffer, from my own bad choices.

Well, Mother. I've been writing a long time. There's so much yet to say. But I think I'll stop for now. My wrist is tired from writing. And I have, still, a life to live. My friend asked me if I thought I'd ever stop thinking about you, wondering, wishing. I answered that I didn't think I could. Because we are tied, like it or not, as closely as two human beings can be, by that umbilical cord. Forever and ever linked. In life, and in death, too. Mother. Daughter.

Episode 21

Solace

It is the last day of my visit, my last day in the old Vermont inn, a day with my best friend's daughter, now almost forty years old, older than her mother was when she had died; with my best friend's son, last seen by me when he was four, now with his sweet wife and their little girl and little boy — my best friend's grandchildren.

My friend's daughter came to get me this morning where I waited outside on the inn steps and drove me to see her brother and his family, then later to the farm where her father still lived — the rooms in that house, where I spent that last day with my friend, looked just the same, and as we sat outside on the deck in the sun, her daughter in dark sunglasses, shining dark hair so much like her mother's, I felt transposed back in time — her voice even sounded like her mother's voice. So the past, in its ways, does come back, even when I don't write about it.

When we left the farm it was dusk. The earth around us was in early spring, only a few weeks later than the last time I was there, long ago, the season known as "unlocking" season. The road was narrow, unpaved, bumpy, with the sound of gravel against the wheels, and of branches of the trees in these wooded acres around the farm scraping against the car.

My friend's daughter said, "I'm glad you came." When I heard her say that, I felt a letting-go, a feeling that I had in some way been able to keep my promise to her mother. It was as if all three of us were there in that car in that moment, near my friend's farm, near where she lay in her grave.

Back at the Vermont inn, because it was night time, the lamps were all glowing in the lobby living room. I headed up the stairs to my room. At seventy, I am weary, I am no longer young, and I needed to go to bed.

I was pleased that in my room there was an old beauty of a secretary desk, but when I opened it to place its writing surface down to write these final thoughts, I saw that it was broken inside, dusty, not likely to have been used by any earlier guests, because people don't write much by hand these days.

I hear that cursive writing is no longer even taught in school, and few people use a fountain pen, like my blue one, which has run out of ink and so I'm using a blotchy ballpoint. But writing, even with a bad pen, is still my listening friend, my counselor, my lamp.

This antique walnut desk with cubbyholes, this secretary desk, is almost exactly like the one I used as a child, the one that was in Mother's room before I was old enough to have it in my own. It was my great-grandmother's desk, which still bears a black burn on its edge where Mother had once carelessly left a cigarette. I'm saving it to pass on to my granddaughter when she's old enough to write.

Afterword

A Life in Diaries

One April day when I am seventy-six, I take my favorite place in the library—a chair at the end of the long wooden table that is closest to the tall windows, through which I can see the branches of trees—and turn on one of the green reading lamps. Now I wait. Soon a reference librarian rolls to my table a beige metal cart whose shelf holds four boxes (the at-a-time limit) of the thirty-two boxes of my archived diaries; spiral-bound notebooks of various sizes in which I have recorded, daily, much of the past forty-two years of my life.

This is the thirteenth trip I have made from my home in Illinois to the Arthur and Elizabeth Schlesinger Library on the History of Women in America in Cambridge, Massachusetts, to visit my past in my diaries. For me, especially, because I never had Mother's loving attention, to have my diaries valued and preserved in this library—even though no one but me will read them until 2070—is a mighty balm.

The Schlesinger's purpose is to "illuminate the lives of American women past and present" and among their collections are many diaries. Included are Mother's girlhood diaries from 1911,

1921, 1925, and 1927, which, as I wrote in my memoir, *Missing*, I brought here twenty years ago. The library also accepted, in addition to those and to my own diaries, letters, photographs, and other papers from my family, my book manuscripts about miscarriage and about adoption, and other papers about my social work activities, almost all of which are open to researchers.

On this thirteenth visit to the Schlesinger, I stay for four nights where I have always stayed—at a guest house that is a pleasant walking distance from the library, across Harvard Yard. The guest house is practical, modest yet comfortable, and my room has an armchair and a table for a desk. In this old, quiet house, I, and the other guests—mostly solitary, purposeful-looking women—slip quietly in and out of our rooms and the common breakfast area, the same way I slip in and out of the past in my days at the library.

I sleep each night happy, because it is only for a few nights, to be alone—silent, beyond the reach of The World, in my comfortable bed by a partly open window, through which I hear, in the morning, birdsong. I rise and stretch, in a morning that is just for me, in which I will travel back in my life, to the years when, as a mother, I woke always into others' needs.

Each morning I walk to the library and read in these note-books, sitting at the table, and sometimes standing up to ease my back. The hours pass; the sun fades and clouds move in. In my diaries I see how moods, upsets, happiness, and unhappiness, can change, and then, like the weather, change again. I tran-scribe some paragraphs that I may use in another writing pro-ject, but mostly, on this trip, I enjoy the peculiar and satisfying feeling of reliving the past, even when what I read disturbs me, because all of it belongs to the precious years of my one-and-only life.

Pressed between the pages of one of my diaries I find a flower. Also reminders from AA friends in response to too much worry about my children or life: "Are they safe today?" and "Are you sober today?" I read the advice of a singing teacher from those summer weeks we spent in Italy long ago: "You must go serenely and without fear to find your voice." And of a dream that I got something fixed that my parents lived with forever un-fixed: it needed one screw.

By four o'clock, I've had enough for the day, and joke to the librarian, "Take them back to the nursery!" and she smiles as she rolls the cart with my boxes of diaries back into the library office. I am remembering the two occasions when a nurse rolled a cart to me with my newborn son, then my newborn daughter. These pages, these thousands of words, I have also given birth to.

I pack up my things and leave the library, leaving my past behind and walking back in the present to the guest house, no longer that younger woman who wrote those early diaries, but a grandmother of four. I stop at a corner store to buy a cold plate of food to take back for my dinner, which I will eat, with tea, in the guest house common area, reading the newspaper, then re-treat to my room to read, to call my husband, perhaps to listen to music on my phone.

My diaries have given me, in a way, an additional life. Being able to visit, again, those dear, ordinary days, which Time strings together like beads to form a life, helps me remember to value each present day. But why do it at all? I have written my diaries because I wanted to leave a handprint on the cave wall, to say,

"I was here. This is what it was like for me to be alive in this time and this place." And because writing is and has been my listening friend, my counselor, my lamp. My solace.

ACKNOWLEDGMENTS

Grateful thanks to Jennifer Harris, David Wesley Williams, Kristen Weber, Reginald Gibbons, Laura Marie PR, Suzanne Frischkorn, Naomi Shihab Nye, Jenny Gotwals, Kathy Jacob and the staff of the Arthur and Elizabeth Schlesinger Library on the History of Women in America.

JACKLEG PRESS

V. Joshua Adams, Scott Shibuya Brown, Michael Chin, Chloe Clark, Brian Rivka Clifton, Brittney Corrigan, Jessica Cuello, Barbara Cully, Alison Cundiff, Neil de la Flor, Suzanne Frischkorn, Victoria Garza, Reginald Gibbons, Joachim Glage, Caroline Goodwin, Kathryn Kruse, Brigitte Lewis, Jenny Magnus, D.K. McCutchen, Jean McGarry, Rita Mookerjee, Mamie Morgan, Alexis Orgera, Karen Rigby, Jo Salas, Maureen Seaton, Kristine Snodgrass, Cornelia Maude Spelman, Peter Stenson, Melissa Studdard, Curious Theatre, Gemini Wahhaj, Megan Weiler, Cassandra Whitaker, David Wesley Williams

jacklegpress.org

A MEMOIR

Cornelia Maude Spelman

MISSING

BOOKS BY
CORNELIA MAUDE SPELMAN

Missing

FOR CHILDREN:

After Charlotte's Mom Died
Your Body Belongs to You
Mama and Daddy Bear's Divorce
When I Feel Angry
When I Feel Scared
When I Feel Sad
When I Feel Jealous
When I Feel Good about Myself
When I Miss You
When I Feel Worried
When I Care about Others
Everybody's Somewhere
A Foot Is Not a Fish!

Cornelia's papers at the Schlesinger Library
on the History of Women in America
https://id.lib.harvard.edu/alma/990091861930203941/catalog

www.corneliaspelman.com

Printed in the USA
CPSIA information can be obtained
at www.ICGtesting.com
JSHW020718060624
64369JS00003B/5